Better Homes and Gardens®

MAKE·A·MEAL SALADS

Our seal assures you that every recipe in *Make-a-Meal Salads*
has been tested in the Better Homes and Gardens® Test Kitchen.
This means that each recipe is practical and reliable, and
meets our high standards of taste appeal.

BETTER HOMES AND GARDENS₀ BOOKS

Editor: Gerald M. Knox
Art Director: Ernest Shelton
Managing Editor: David A. Kirchner
Copy and Production Editors: James D. Blume, Marsha Jahns,
    Rosanne Weber Mattson, Mary Helen Schiltz

Food and Nutrition Editor: Nancy Byal
Department Head, Cook Books: Sharyl Heiken
Associate Department Heads: Sandra Granseth,
    Rosemary C. Hutchinson, Elizabeth Woolever
Senior Food Editors: Julia Malloy, Marcia Stanley, Joyce Trollope
Associate Food Editors: Linda Henry, Mary Jo Plutt,
    Maureen Powers, Martha Schiel, Linda Foley Woodrum
Recipe Development Editor: Marion Viall
Test Kitchen Director: Sharon Stilwell
Test Kitchen Photo Studio Director: Janet Pittman
Test Kitchen Home Economists: Jean Brekke, Kay Cargill,
    Marilyn Cornelius, Jennifer Darling, Maryellyn Krantz,
    Lynelle Munn, Dianna Nolin, Marge Steenson, Cynthia Volcko

Associate Art Directors: Linda Ford Vermie, Neoma Alt West,
    Randall Yontz
Assistant Art Directors: Lynda Haupert, Harijs Priekulis,
    Tom Wegner
Senior Graphic Designers: Jack Murphy, Stan Sams,
    Darla Whipple-Frain
Graphic Designers: Mike Burns, Sally Cooper, Blake Welch,
    Brian Wignall, Kimberly Zarley

Vice President, Editorial Director: Doris Eby
Executive Director, Editorial Services: Duane L. Gregg

Senior Vice President, General Manager: Fred Stines
Director of Publishing: Robert B. Nelson
Vice President, Retail Marketing: Jamie Martin
Vice President, Direct Marketing: Arthur Heydendael

MAKE-A-MEAL SALADS

Editor: Mary Jo Plutt
Copy and Production Editor: James D. Blume
Graphic Designer: Jack Murphy
Electronic Text Processor: Joyce Wasson
Contributing Photographers: Ernie Block Studio, Scott Little
Food Stylist: Janet Pittman
Contributing Illustrator: Thomas Rosborough

On the front cover: Steak Salads
(see recipe, page 59)

Not too many years ago, few cooks would have thought of serving a salad as a main dish. Salads then were just part of the mealtime's supporting cast. Today's cooks, though, conscious of their families' health and the need for variety, are beginning to accept that salads can fit fine in the starring role, too.

As I wrote *Make-a-Meal Salads,* I had one major goal: to give you and your family page after page of the most creative salad ideas you've ever seen.

To achieve this goal, I started with some old-time family-favorite salads and added new twists. Recipes such as Garden Potato Salad with Ham and Wilted Lettuce with Chicken were the delicious results. Then I branched out even further, taking traditional main dishes like paella and pizza and turning them into Paella Salad and Deep-Dish Salad Pizza.

Now it's your turn to discover the wonderful world of salads. Soon you'll hear, "Salad for dinner? ... What a great idea!"

Mary Jo Plato

THE MAKING OF A SALAD 6

Here are the answers to questions on selecting, handling, and identifying salad greens.

MIXING-IT-UP SALADS 13

Put your ingredients in a bowl and toss them together—it's that easy.

ARRANGED OR LAYERED SALADS 43

Discover the secrets for simple yet beautiful arrangements.

MARINATED OR MOLDED SALADS 57

No time for last-minute cooking? Marinated or molded salads are wonderful make-aheads.

SALADS-IN-A-SHELL 65

Try fresh pineapples, melons, tomatoes, and even tortilla and pastry shells as "bowls" for your salads.

DRESSING IT UP 77

You'll be the toast of the town when family and friends taste your homemade vinaigrettes, flavored vinegars and oils, creamy dressings, and salad toppers.

SALAD BUFFET PARTY 88

A feast of main-dish salads, soups, and rolls.

INDEX 94

The Making of a Salad

Proper preparation and freshness—they're the key ingredients in any salad. For hints on preparing salad greens, take a look at these two pages. To learn more about how to judge freshness and how to identify salad greens, turn to pages 8–12.

Cleaning the greens
Clean the greens before storing them. Before washing the greens, remove and discard any outer leaves that are bruised, discolored, tough, or wilted.

Loosen the core from iceberg lettuce by hitting the stem end sharply on a countertop. Then twist the core and lift it out. Don't use a sharp knife to remove the core because the cut edges of iceberg lettuce will turn a rusty color.

Wash iceberg lettuce by placing the core side up under cold running water. Rinse the lettuce thoroughly, then invert the head and let the water run out.

To clean other large-leaf salad greens, such as Bibb lettuce, romaine, and curly endive, cut the bottom core off. Then wash the leaves under cold running water.

Greens with small leaves, such as spinach, watercress, and arugula, should be dunked in a large bowl of cool water. It's important to wash the greens thoroughly

Cleaning

Drying

to remove any dirt and sand particles. After a few minutes, lift the greens out and discard the water. Repeat the dunking of the greens until no more sand collects in the bottom of the bowl.

You'll want to use only the tender leaves from the greens when making a salad. So break off and discard the stems from spinach, Swiss chard, sorrel, and mustard greens; cut out the heavy midrib from romaine; and use only the leaves from arugula and watercress.

Drying the greens
Water on the greens dilutes the salad dressing and prevents the dressing from

basket and then turn the handle to spin the basket. As the basket turns, much of the moisture spins out. But you may still need to blot the leaves dry with a towel.

Crisping and storing greens
If the greens are a little limp, crisp the leaves by putting them in a clear plastic bag while they're still slightly damp. Then refrigerate them for at least eight hours.

Always refrigerate greens until you're ready to use them. When properly stored, greens will stay crisp for as long as three or four days. For most greens, store the leaves in a clear plastic bag or an airtight container.

Tearing greens
Unless a salad calls for shredded lettuce or cabbage, don't cut the greens. Instead, tear the leaves into bite-size pieces. Tearing causes less bruising to the leaves. It also exposes more of the insides of the leaves, which absorb the salad dressing better.

Adding the dressing
A salad dressing should enhance a salad, so add only enough to *lightly* coat the leaves. Too much dressing will mask the other flavors in the salad; too little will leave the salad tasteless.

After the dressing has been added, use two salad servers or spoons to toss the salad.

Crisping and storing

Tearing

Adding the dressing

clinging to the leaves. So after draining the greens, remove as much moisture from them as possible.

An easy way to dry the greens is to place the leaves on paper towels or a clean kitchen towel. Place a second towel over them, then gently pat them dry.

A salad spinner also works well to dry greens. Place small or torn leaves in the

Arugula and watercress need to be stored differently than the other greens. Never store arugula when it's damp because it will turn yellow and rot quickly.

Watercress absorbs water through its stems rather than its leaves. After washing watercress, stand the stems up in a container of water. Cover the leaves loosely with a plastic bag and refrigerate.

Gently push downward to the bottom of the bowl with one salad server and lift up and over with the other server. Don't be too enthusiastic when tossing the salad or you'll bruise the tender leaves.

For arranged salads, you can either drizzle the salad dressing over the top of the arrangement or pass the dressing separately.

Leaf lettuce

Radicchio

Sorrel

Leaf lettuce comes in two forms. The first is a stem lettuce which grows as single leaves. The second grows in loose heads with the leaves branching from a stalk. The long ruffled leaves of leaf lettuce are either completely green or green with reddish bronze tips. Leaf lettuce is a tender, mild lettuce that contrasts nicely with crisp greens in a salad.

Sorrel (SAW-ruhl) has a pleasant lemony flavor which complements fish well in a main-dish salad. Small pieces of sorrel can add a bright green contrast when mixed with Bibb, Boston, or leaf lettuce. For a crisp yet tender texture, use only the small leaves. The woody stems are undesirable.

Radicchio (rah-DEE-kee-oh) is an Italian term for all chicories. The radicchio we know is the red Verona chicory. It grows in small, round, compact heads. The leaves are ruby red with thick, white veins. Eaten alone, it's quite bitter. But mixed with other greens and tossed with a vinaigrette, it adds a nice accent to a salad.

Iceberg lettuce

Romaine

Butterhead lettuce

Arugula

Iceberg lettuce, sometimes called crisphead lettuce, is the most common type of lettuce. Its compact, round, smooth head consists of crisp, mild-tasting leaves. The leaves range in color from a medium green on the outside of the head to a pale green on the inside. You can tear iceberg lettuce into bite-size pieces, shred it, or cut it into wedges.

Butterhead lettuce grows in small, fluffy, round heads, and has a mild, slightly sweet buttery flavor. The butterhead lettuce varieties are Bibb lettuce and Boston lettuce. Bibb lettuce is slightly darker and has a smaller head than Boston lettuce. Use the torn, tender leaves to add a delicate touch to a tossed salad. Or use the cup-shaped leaves from the head as individual bowls for your salad.

Romaine or cos has long, dark green leaves that branch from a white base. Try the crisp, slightly sharp-flavored leaves alone or with other greens in a salad.

Arugula (uh-ROOG-yuh-luh) or rocket has small tender leaves with a peppery flavor similar to horseradish. Combine the leaves with mild greens for a contrasting flavor in a salad.

9

Escarole

Mustard greens

Spinach

Mustard greens add a peppery accent when used sparingly in a lettuce or spinach salad. Use only the small, young leaves in a salad. They'll be more tender than the older leaves. The older leaves are better used in cooking.

Escarole (ES-kuh-rohl) is also known as broadleaf endive. It comes from the same family as curly endive, but is less frilly. The leaves of escarole are broad, flat, and only slightly curled. The firm, chewy texture and slightly bitter flavor of escarole blend well with iceberg lettuce and with mild, creamy dressings.

Spinach, in both its curly and flat-leaf forms, is well known as a tasty vegetable—whether cooked or eaten raw in a salad. Try the slightly bitter, dark green chewy leaves alone or mixed with other salad greens.

10

Swiss chard

Curly endive

Watercress

Belgian endive

Curly endive, also known as chicory, has frilly, narrow, dark green leaves. Curly endive grows in large clumps that look like small bushes or shrubs. The chewy leaves and pleasantly bitter tang are a welcome change from the bland lettuces.

Watercress adds a lively, peppery tang to a salad. The small, delicate, dark green leaves have a short storage life, so try to use them soon after you buy them.

Belgian endive is also known as witloof chicory. It has 5- to 6-inch-long tender leaves with a mild, sweet flavor. The leaves should be creamy white to pale yellow at the tips. Once exposed to light, Belgian endive begins to turn green and lose its delicate flavor.

Swiss chard or chard has a celerylike rib with a dark green leaf that fans out into a spinachlike top. Use the large, coarse leaves to line salad bowls. Or mix the torn leaves with spinach for added bite to a salad.

Red cabbage

Chinese cabbage

Savoy cabbage

Green cabbage

Cabbage adds a delicate, fresh flavor to salads.

The three major types of head cabbage are savoy, green, and red. Savoy has crinkly leaves and is slightly milder in flavor than either the green or the red.

Cabbage usually is sold with its outer leaves (called wrapper leaves) trimmed off to expose the pale inner leaves. Be sure to look for heads that are heavy for their size and ones that show no discoloration.

To use cabbage in a salad such as coleslaw, shred it. Or use the larger leaves as "cups" for individual salad servings.

Chinese cabbage, also known as napa cabbage or celery cabbage, grows on a celerylike stalk. Actually, it is not a member of the head cabbage family. The slightly frilly, pale leaves have the flavor of both celery and cabbage. Use torn leaves or thinly sliced stems to add crunch to your salad.

12

MIXING·IT·UP

Tossed salads—
versatile, delicious, and
simple to prepare. Whatever
the occasion—a picnic in
the park or an elegant dinner
party—these easy-to-make
lettuce, vegetable, and pasta
salads are sure to please.

Salad-Making Hints

What's a Cup?

Most ingredients in our recipes call for cup measures. But when you're shopping, how much should you buy? Here's a guide to help you in your planning.

Ingredient	Amount Before Preparation	Approximate Measure After Preparation
Bibb lettuce	1 medium head (5 ounces)	3 cups torn
Boston lettuce	1 medium head (8 ounces)	5 cups torn
Broccoli	1 pound	3½ cups flowerets
Cabbage	1 small head (1 pound)	5 cups shredded
Carrots	2 medium (5 ounces)	1 cup sliced
Cauliflower	1 medium head (1½ pounds)	4 cups flowerets
Celery	1 stalk	½ cup sliced
Cheese	4 ounces	1 cup shredded
Cucumber	1 medium (8 ounces)	1¾ cups sliced *or* 1¼ cups chopped
Green onions with tops	1 bunch (7 medium)	½ cup sliced
Green pepper	1 large	1 cup chopped
Iceberg lettuce	1 small head (15 ounces)	7½ cups torn *or* 8 cups shredded
Meat, cooked	1 pound	3 cups chopped
Mushrooms	16 large (8 ounces)	3 cups sliced
Radishes	12 medium (4 ounces)	1 cup sliced
Romaine	1 medium head (1 pound)	10 cups torn
Sorrel	4 ounces	5½ cups torn
Spinach	1 pound	12 cups torn
Tomato	1 medium (6 ounces)	1 cup chopped
Watercress	4 ounces	2 cups leaves only
Zucchini	1 medium (8 ounces)	2 cups sliced

Mediterranean Salad

The yogurt in the meatballs adds a flavor bonus.

1 egg
⅓ cup plain yogurt
¾ cup soft bread crumbs
    (1 slice)
½ teaspoon salt
¼ teaspoon ground allspice
1 pound ground beef *or*
    ground lamb
6 cups torn romaine
1½ cups cherry tomatoes,
    halved
1 cup sliced radishes
½ cup sliced green onion
1 2¼-ounce can sliced pitted
    ripe olives, drained
⅓ cup salad oil
¼ cup lemon juice
1 teaspoon dried mint,
    crushed
¼ cup crumbled feta cheese

● In a large mixing bowl beat egg, then add yogurt. Stir in bread crumbs, salt, and allspice. Add ground beef or lamb and mix well. Shape mixture into 1-inch meatballs. Place meatballs in a 15x10x1-inch baking pan.

● Bake, uncovered, in a 350° oven about 15 minutes or till done. Remove meatballs from pan and drain on paper towels. Cool meatballs slightly.

● Meanwhile, in a very large salad bowl combine romaine, tomatoes, radishes, onion, and olives. Cover and chill while preparing dressing. For dressing, in a screw-top jar combine oil, lemon juice, and mint. Cover and shake well.

● For salad, add meatballs to lettuce mixture. Shake dressing again and pour it over lettuce mixture. Toss lightly to coat. Sprinkle salad with feta cheese. Makes 6 servings.

Stir-Fried Beef Salad

Here's a salad you make using a wok.

¾ pound beef round steak
¼ cup clear Italian
    salad dressing
3 cups torn spinach
1 cup sliced fresh mushrooms
1 small cucumber, seeded
    and coarsely chopped
1 large tomato, cut into
    wedges
1 medium onion, sliced and
    separated into rings
½ of a medium green pepper,
    seeded and cut into strips
1 tablespoon cooking oil
⅓ cup clear Italian
    salad dressing

● Trim any excess fat from steak. Partially freeze the steak, then cut on the bias into thin bite-size strips. Place meat in a small mixing bowl.

● Pour the ¼ cup dressing over meat and toss lightly to coat. Let stand at room temperature for 30 minutes.

● In a large salad bowl combine spinach, mushrooms, cucumber, tomato, onion, and green pepper. Cover and chill while cooking the meat.

● Drain meat and discard dressing. Preheat a wok or a large skillet over high heat. Add cooking oil. Stir-fry the meat for 2 to 3 minutes or till brown. Remove from heat.

● Immediately add hot beef and ⅓ cup dressing to spinach mixture. Toss lightly to coat. Makes 4 servings.

Garden Potato Salad with Ham

Orange 'n' Kiwi Salad

Choose your largest bowl to give plenty of room for tossing. Then, for an attractive presentation, transfer the salad to a smaller lettuce-lined bowl and top with sprouts.

  5 ounces jicama *or* one
     8-ounce can sliced water
     chestnuts, drained
  6 cups torn romaine
1½ cups cubed cooked beef
  3 oranges, peeled and
     sectioned
  2 kiwi fruits, peeled, halved
     lengthwise, and sliced
  2 stalks celery, thinly sliced
  1 small red onion, thinly
     sliced and separated into
     rings
  ¼ cup walnut oil *or* salad oil
  ½ teaspoon *each* finely
     shredded orange peel *and*
     lemon peel
  ¼ cup orange juice
  2 tablespoons lemon juice
  1 teaspoon sugar

● If using jicama, peel it and cut it into 2-inch julienne sticks. (You should have about 1 cup.) In a very large salad bowl combine jicama or drained water chestnuts, romaine, beef, orange sections, kiwi fruits, celery, and onion. Cover and chill while preparing the dressing.

● For dressing, in a screw-top jar combine walnut oil or salad oil, orange peel, lemon peel, orange juice, lemon juice, sugar, and dash *salt.* Cover and shake well. Pour the dressing over romaine mixture. Toss lightly to coat. Makes 4 servings.

Garden Potato Salad with Ham

1¾ pounds whole tiny new
     potatoes
  ⅔ cup chopped carrot
  1 medium zucchini, cut into
     bite-size sticks
2½ cups cubed fully cooked
     ham
  2 tablespoons thinly sliced
     green onion
1¼ cups mayonnaise *or* salad
     dressing
  2 teaspoons sugar
  2 teaspoons celery seed
  2 teaspoons vinegar
  2 teaspoons prepared
     mustard
  2 hard-cooked eggs, coarsely
     chopped
     Sliced zucchini (optional)

● In a large covered saucepan cook potatoes in boiling water for 12 to 15 minutes or till tender, then drain. Rinse with cold water, then drain again. Slice potatoes and set aside.

● Meanwhile, in another covered saucepan cook carrot in a small amount of boiling water for 2 minutes. Add zucchini sticks and cook about 2 minutes more or till vegetables are nearly tender, then drain. Rinse with cold water. Drain again.

● In a large mixing bowl combine potatoes, carrot, zucchini sticks, ham, and green onion.

● For dressing, stir together mayonnaise or salad dressing, sugar, celery seed, vinegar, mustard, and ½ teaspoon *salt.* Pour dressing over potato mixture. Toss lightly to coat. Carefully fold in the chopped eggs. Cover and chill for 4 hours or overnight.

● To serve, spoon about ¾ of the potato salad into a serving bowl. If desired, overlap zucchini slices around edge of bowl. Finish spooning in the remaining salad. Makes 6 servings.

Vegetable-Ham Medley Salad

A salad so colorful you can skip the garnish.

1 cup fresh *or* frozen peas
2 cups cooked rice
1 cup cubed fully cooked ham
   or cooked pork
4 ounces cheddar cheese,
   cubed
¾ cup chopped celery
½ cup chopped green pepper
2 tablespoons snipped chives
   or green onion tops
3 tablespoons white wine
   vinegar
3 tablespoons olive oil *or*
   salad oil
1½ teaspoons snipped fresh
   basil *or* chervil, *or*
   ½ teaspoon dried basil
   or chervil, crushed
   Leaf lettuce

● In a small covered saucepan cook fresh peas in a small amount of lightly salted boiling water about 5 minutes or till tender, then drain. (Or cook frozen peas according to package directions, then drain.) Rinse with cold water, then drain again.

● In a medium mixing bowl combine the cooked peas, rice, ham or pork, cheese, celery, green pepper, and chives or green onion tops. Toss lightly to mix. Cover and chill till serving time.

● For dressing, in a screw-top jar combine vinegar, oil, basil or chervil, ¼ teaspoon *salt,* and ⅛ teaspoon *pepper.* Cover and shake well. Chill till serving time.

● To serve, shake dressing and pour it over rice mixture. Toss lightly to coat. Line 4 salad plates with lettuce leaves. Spoon rice mixture onto the plates. Makes 4 servings.

Cheese Macaroni Salad

Surprise! Use a simple macaroni-and-cheese dinner mix as the base for this pasta salad.

1 7¼-ounce package
   macaroni-and-
   cheese dinner mix
1 9-ounce package frozen
   Italian green beans
1½ cups milk
1½ teaspoons dried basil,
   crushed
8 ounces fully cooked ham,
   cut into bite-size julienne
   strips (about 1½ cups)
½ cup pitted ripe olives, halved
½ cup dairy sour cream
½ cup mayonnaise *or* salad
   dressing
2 tablespoons snipped parsley
1 tablespoon Dijon-style
   mustard
⅛ teaspoon onion powder
   Romaine leaves
   Small tomato wedges

● In a large saucepan cook macaroni from dinner mix in 6 cups boiling *water* for 5 minutes. Add beans and return to boiling. Boil gently, covered, for 4 to 5 minutes more or till macaroni and beans are tender. Drain.

● Stir cheese sauce mix from dinner mix, milk, and basil into macaroni and beans in saucepan. Cook over medium heat about 5 minutes or till slightly thickened and bubbly. Cook and stir for 1 minute more. Remove from heat and cool slightly, stirring once or twice.

● In a large mixing bowl combine macaroni mixture, ham, and olives. In a small mixing bowl stir together sour cream, mayonnaise or salad dressing, parsley, mustard, and onion powder. Pour sour cream mixture over macaroni mixture. Toss lightly to coat. Cover and chill the mixture for 6 hours or overnight.

● To serve, if necessary, stir in several tablespoons of additional *milk* to moisten mixture. Line 4 salad plates with lettuce leaves. Spoon macaroni mixture onto the plates. Garnish with tomato wedges. Makes 4 servings.

Grape and Pork Salad

The almonds add an extra crunch. Toast them in a 350° oven about 10 minutes or until they're light brown.

4	cups torn Bibb lettuce *or* Boston lettuce
2	cups torn romaine
2	cups seedless red grapes, halved
1½	cups cooked pork cut into julienne strips
3	tablespoons olive oil *or* salad oil
2	tablespoons water
2	tablespoons wine vinegar
¾	teaspoon ground coriander
½	teaspoon sugar
¼	teaspoon garlic salt
¼	cup slivered almonds, toasted

● In a very large mixing bowl combine the Bibb or Boston lettuce, romaine, grapes, and pork. Cover and chill while preparing the dressing.

● For dressing, in a screw-top jar combine olive oil or salad oil, water, vinegar, coriander, sugar, and garlic salt. Cover and shake well. Pour over lettuce mixture. Toss lightly to coat.

● To serve, spoon mixture onto 4 salad plates. Sprinkle with almonds. Makes 4 servings.

Tabbouleh with Lamb

Tabbouleh (tuh-BOO-luh) is a refreshing Middle Eastern salad featuring bulgur (a Turkish wheat). Chill the salad for several hours so the wheat soaks up the sensational mint dressing.

8	ounces cooked lamb *or* chicken
⅓	cup salad oil
⅓	cup lemon juice
2	tablespoons snipped fresh mint *or* 2 teaspoons dried mint, crushed
½	teaspoon salt
⅛	teaspoon pepper
2	cloves garlic, minced
2	cups boiling water
1	cup bulgur wheat
½	cup chopped celery
½	cup thinly sliced carrot
½	cup snipped parsley
¼	cup chopped green pepper
¼	cup sliced green onion
1¼	cups finely chopped cucumber
2	medium tomatoes, chopped Leaf lettuce

● If using lamb, trim any excess fat from it. Chop the lamb or chicken and place the meat in a large bowl. (You should have about 1½ cups.)

● For dressing, in a screw-top jar combine oil, lemon juice, mint, salt, pepper, and garlic. Cover and shake well. Pour dressing over meat. Let stand at room temperature for 30 minutes.

● Meanwhile, in a medium mixing bowl combine boiling water and bulgur. Let stand for 20 minutes. Drain well, then squeeze out excess water. Add bulgur, celery, carrot, parsley, green pepper, and onion to meat mixture. Toss lightly to coat. Cover and chill for 3 to 5 hours.

● To serve, stir in cucumber and tomatoes. Line 6 salad plates with lettuce leaves. Spoon bulgur mixture onto the plates. Makes 6 servings.

Create-a-Chef's Salad

Create your own salad by choosing your favorite luncheon meat and dressing.

3 cups torn iceberg lettuce
3 cups torn romaine
2 tomatoes, cut into wedges
1½ cups desired cold cuts cut into julienne strips
4 ounces American, cheddar, *or* Swiss cheese, cubed
½ of a small cucumber, sliced
½ of a small red onion, sliced and separated into rings
½ of a green pepper, cut into rings
3 hard-cooked eggs, sliced
Desired salad dressing

● In a very large mixing bowl combine iceberg lettuce, romaine, tomatoes, meat, cheese, cucumber, onion, and green pepper. Toss lightly to mix.

● To serve, spoon lettuce mixture onto 6 salad plates. Garnish with egg slices. Serve with desired salad dressing. Serves 6.

Deli-Style Pasta Salad

1 7-ounce package corkscrew macaroni
6 ounces provolone cheese, cut into ¾-inch cubes
6 ounces sliced Genoa salami, cut into strips
1 small zucchini, thinly sliced
1 small onion, thinly sliced and separated into rings
½ cup chopped green pepper *or* sweet red pepper
1 2¼-ounce can sliced pitted ripe olives, drained
¼ cup grated Parmesan cheese
¼ cup snipped parsley
½ cup olive oil
¼ cup white wine vinegar
1½ teaspoons dry mustard
1 teaspoon dried oregano, crushed
1 teaspoon dried basil, crushed
1 clove garlic, minced
2 medium tomatoes, cut into wedges
Parsley sprigs (optional)

● Cook macaroni according to package directions, then drain. Rinse with cold water, then drain again.

● In a large mixing bowl combine macaroni, provolone cheese, salami, zucchini, onion, green or red pepper, olives, Parmesan cheese, and snipped parsley.

● For dressing, in a screw-top jar combine olive oil, vinegar, dry mustard, oregano, basil, and garlic. Cover and shake well. Pour dressing over pasta mixture and toss lightly to coat. Cover and chill for 4 hours or overnight.

● To serve, add tomato wedges and toss lightly. Transfer pasta mixture to a large salad bowl. If desired, garnish with parsley sprigs. Makes 8 servings.

Deli-Style Pasta Salad

Asparagus-Brats Toss

This recipe has all the makings of the perfect potluck food—it's easy to tote and can be made up to 24 hours ahead.

4 ounces spaghetti ½ teaspoon dried basil, crushed ½ teaspoon dried thyme, crushed 10 ounces fresh asparagus, *or* one 8- *or* 10-ounce package frozen cut asparagus 12 ounces cooked bratwurst, bias-sliced into ¼-inch slices 2 small tomatoes, cut into wedges ¼ cup sliced green onion ½ cup creamy Italian salad dressing Milk Grated Parmesan cheese	● Break spaghetti into 2-inch-long pieces. Cook the spaghetti according to package directions, then drain. Rinse with cold water, then drain again. Place spaghetti in a large salad bowl. Add basil and thyme, then toss lightly to mix. Set mixture aside. ● Cut fresh asparagus into 1-inch pieces. In a medium covered saucepan cook fresh asparagus in a small amount of lightly salted boiling water for 8 to 10 minutes or till nearly tender, then drain. (Or cook frozen asparagus according to package directions, then drain.) Rinse with cold water. Drain again. ● Add asparagus, bratwurst, tomatoes, and green onion to spaghetti mixture. Pour dressing over spaghetti mixture and toss lightly to coat. Cover and chill for 3 to 24 hours. ● To serve, if necessary, add a few tablespoons of milk and toss spaghetti mixture lightly to moisten mixture. Sprinkle with Parmesan cheese. Makes 4 servings.

Hot Potato and Bratwurst Salad

Here's a Test Kitchen tip: If tiny new potatoes are unavailable, cube three medium potatoes and cook them for 10 to 15 minutes in the lightly salted boiling water.

1 pound whole tiny new potatoes, each cut into eight wedges 2 slices bacon 12 ounces smoked bratwurst *or* knackwurst, bias-sliced into ¼-inch slices ⅓ cup chopped onion ¼ cup sliced celery 1 tablespoon sugar 1½ teaspoons cornstarch ¼ teaspoon salt ¼ teaspoon celery seed Dash pepper ⅓ cup water 3 tablespoons vinegar Snipped parsley	● In a large covered saucepan cook potatoes in lightly salted boiling water for 8 to 10 minutes or just till tender. Drain the potatoes and set aside. ● In a 10-inch skillet cook bacon till crisp. Remove bacon from skillet, reserving 1 tablespoon drippings. Crumble bacon and set aside. In the skillet cook bratwurst or knackwurst, onion, and celery in the reserved drippings till meat is light brown and vegetables are tender, stirring occasionally. ● In a small mixing bowl combine the sugar, cornstarch, salt, celery seed, and pepper. Stir in water and vinegar. Pour over bratwurst mixture in skillet. Cook and stir till thickened and bubbly. Add the potatoes and bacon. Continue cooking for 3 to 5 minutes more or till potatoes are heated through, tossing lightly to coat. Sprinkle with parsley. Makes 4 servings.

Brown Bagger's Salad

Pack two of these salads along with some crackers, and you and a friend can enjoy a pleasant lunch without leaving the office.

¾ cup shredded cabbage
½ of a small tomato, seeded and chopped
¼ cup cream-style cottage cheese, drained
¼ cup chopped seeded cucumber
1 slice turkey breast luncheon meat, cut into 1½-inch julienne strips
1 slice (1½ ounces) cheddar cheese, cut into 1½-inch julienne sticks
2 tablespoons desired salad dressing

● In a small mixing bowl combine cabbage, tomato, cottage cheese, cucumber, turkey, and cheddar cheese. Toss lightly to mix. Pour desired salad dressing over cabbage mixture. Toss lightly again to coat. Spoon mixture into an airtight container. Cover and chill overnight.

● In the morning, pack the container of *chilled* cabbage mixture in an insulated lunch box with an ice pack. Serves 1.

Wild Rice with Duck Salad

⅓ cup wild rice
1½ cups water
⅓ cup long grain rice
1½ cups chopped cooked domestic duckling* *or* turkey
2 oranges, peeled and sectioned
1 stalk celery, bias sliced
½ cup snipped parsley
¼ cup sliced green onion
¼ cup walnut oil *or* salad oil
3 tablespoons frozen orange juice concentrate, thawed
1 tablespoon cider vinegar
1 tablespoon Dijon-style mustard
½ cup broken walnuts
Red leaf lettuce
4 orange twists

● Run cold water over *uncooked* wild rice in a strainer for 1 minute, lifting rice with your fingers to rinse well. In a medium saucepan combine wild rice and water. Bring to boiling, then reduce heat. Cover and simmer for 20 minutes. Stir in long grain rice. Return to boiling, then reduce heat. Cover and simmer about 20 minutes more or till rice is tender. Cool rice slightly. In a large mixing bowl combine the warm rice, duckling or turkey, orange sections, celery, parsley, and onion.

● For dressing, in a screw-top jar combine oil, orange juice, vinegar, mustard, ¼ teaspoon *salt,* and ¼ teaspoon *cracked pepper.* Cover and shake well. Pour dressing over rice mixture and toss lightly. Cover and chill for 4 hours or overnight.

● To serve, mix in walnuts. Line 4 salad plates with lettuce leaves. Spoon rice mixture onto the plates. Garnish with orange twists. Makes 4 servings.

*For 1½ to 2 cups of cooked chopped meat, roast a 4½- to 6-pound *domestic duckling.* Place bird, breast up, on a rack in a shallow roasting pan. Prick skin well. Roast, uncovered, in a 375° oven for 40 minutes. Cut band of skin or string between legs. Continue roasting for 20 to 50 minutes more or till drumstick moves easily, spooning off fat occasionally. Cool slightly, then remove skin and bones. Cut up meat as directed in recipe.

Chicken Pocket Sandwiches

Use the tines of a fork to carefully open a pita bread half into a "pocket."

2 cups chopped cabbage
1½ cups chopped cooked
   chicken
1 cup shredded carrot
½ cup broken walnuts
¼ cup chopped radish
⅓ cup mayonnaise *or* salad
   dressing
⅓ cup plain yogurt
2 tablespoons milk
1 tablespoon Dijon-style
   mustard
⅛ teaspoon salt
3 large whole wheat pita bread
   rounds, halved crosswise
½ cup shredded cheddar
   cheese

● In a large mixing bowl combine cabbage, chicken, carrot, walnuts, and radish.

● For dressing, in a small mixing bowl combine mayonnaise or salad dressing, yogurt, milk, mustard, and salt. Stir till well blended. Pour dressing over cabbage mixture and toss lightly to coat. If desired, cover and chill for up to 5 hours.

● To serve, stir cabbage mixture. Spoon mixture into bread halves. Sprinkle with cheese. Makes 3 servings.

Chicken Salad Tacos

A twist to the typical taco! Chicken salad made with sour cream, avocado, olives, and seasonings gives this version a great Mexican flavor.

⅓ cup mayonnaise *or* salad
   dressing
⅓ cup dairy sour cream *or*
   plain yogurt
2 tablespoons chopped onion
2 tablespoons snipped
   cilantro *or* parsley
1 tablespoon lime juice
2 teaspoons taco seasoning
   mix
2½ cups chopped cooked
   chicken *or* turkey
2 medium tomatoes, seeded
   and chopped
¼ cup sliced pitted ripe olives
1½ cups finely shredded iceberg
   lettuce
10 taco shells
1 avocado, seeded, peeled, and
   sliced lengthwise

● In a medium mixing bowl combine mayonnaise or salad dressing, sour cream or yogurt, onion, cilantro or parsley, lime juice, and taco seasoning. Stir in chicken or turkey, tomatoes, and olives. If desired, cover and chill for up to 4 hours.

● To serve, place some lettuce in each taco shell. Spoon chicken mixture on top of lettuce in the shells. Garnish with avocado slices. Makes 5 servings.

Salad Bundles

The outer leaves from a head of iceberg lettuce make the best bundles. They're larger and more flexible than the inner leaves of the head.

1　3-ounce package cream
　　cheese with chives,
　　softened
3　tablespoons mayonnaise *or*
　　salad dressing
¼　teaspoon ground cumin
　　Several dashes bottled hot
　　pepper sauce
2　cups chopped cooked
　　chicken
½　cup shredded carrot
½　cup sliced pitted ripe olives
⅓　cup thinly sliced celery
8　iceberg lettuce leaves

● In a medium mixing bowl stir together cream cheese, mayonnaise or salad dressing, cumin, and hot pepper sauce till well blended. Stir in chicken, carrot, olives, and celery. If desired, cover and chill for up to 8 hours.

● To assemble bundles, cut off the heavy base from each lettuce leaf. Place about ⅓ cup of the chicken mixture in center near base of each leaf. Turn in side edges of lettuce and roll up jelly-roll style. Makes 4 servings.

Making bundles
To assemble the bundles, first take a sharp knife and cut off the heavy base from each lettuce leaf. Place about ⅓ cup of the chicken mixture in the center at the base of each leaf. Turn in the side edges of the lettuce. Starting at the base end, roll up the lettuce and chicken filling jelly-roll style. Then place the bundle with the seam side down on a plate so it doesn't unroll.

Sparkling Strawberry-and-Poultry Salad

Jicamas (HEE-kuh-muhs), of Mexican origin, resemble turnips in shape but have a delicate flavor like water chestnuts.

8 cups torn spinach

2 cups sliced strawberries

8 ounces cooked chicken *or* domestic duckling,* cut into bite-size pieces (about 1½ cups)

5 ounces jicama, peeled and cut into 2-inch julienne sticks (about 1 cup), *or* one 8-ounce can sliced water chestnuts, drained

⅓ cup apricot nectar

¼ cup salad oil

2 tablespoons red wine vinegar *or* Raspberry-Mint Vinegar (see recipe, page 80)

¼ teaspoon sesame oil

¼ cup slivered almonds, toasted

● In a very large salad bowl combine the spinach, strawberries, chicken or duckling, and jicama or water chestnuts. Cover and chill while preparing the dressing.

● For dressing, in a screw-top jar combine apricot nectar, salad oil, vinegar, and sesame oil. Cover and shake well. Pour dressing over spinach mixture and toss lightly to coat. Sprinkle with almonds. Makes 4 servings.

*For the directions on how to roast a domestic duckling, see page 23.

Chicken-Spinach Salad

A salad with a delightful contrast—slightly sweet from the dressing and slightly bitter from the radicchio (rah-DEE-kee-oh).

3 cups torn spinach

1 cup torn radicchio *or* shredded red cabbage

5 ounces cooked chicken *or* turkey, cut into bite-size pieces (1 cup)

¼ of a small onion, thinly sliced and separated into rings

3 tablespoons salad oil

2 tablespoons cider vinegar

2 teaspoons brown sugar

2 slices bacon, crisp-cooked, drained, and crumbled

1 hard-cooked egg, chopped

● In a large mixing bowl combine spinach, radicchio or red cabbage, chicken or turkey, and onion. Cover and chill while preparing the dressing.

● For dressing, in a small bowl combine oil, vinegar, and sugar. Stir till sugar is dissolved. Pour dressing over spinach mixture and toss lightly to coat.

● To serve, spoon spinach mixture onto 2 plates. Sprinkle with crumbled bacon and chopped egg. Makes 2 servings.

Chicken-Spinach Salad

Oriental-Style Chicken Salad

To ensure that they'll puff when you cook them, store the remaining uncooked rice sticks in an airtight container.

Shortening *or* cooking oil for deep-fat frying*
1 ounce rice sticks*
5 cups torn Bibb lettuce *or* Boston lettuce
2 cups chopped cooked chicken
½ of a 6-ounce package (about 1 cup) frozen pea pods, thawed
1 cup sliced fresh mushrooms
⅓ cup salad oil
¼ cup vinegar
2 tablespoons soy sauce
1 tablespoon sugar
⅛ teaspoon ground ginger

● In a 3-quart saucepan or a deep-fat fryer heat 2 inches shortening or cooking oil to 375°. Fry *unsoaked* rice sticks, a few at a time, about 5 seconds or just till sticks puff and rise to the top. Drain on paper towels. Set rice sticks aside. (You should have about 3 cups.)

● In a large salad bowl combine lettuce, chicken, pea pods, and mushrooms. Cover and chill while preparing dressing.

● For dressing, in a screw-top jar combine oil, vinegar, soy sauce, sugar, and ginger. Cover and shake well. Pour dressing over lettuce mixture and toss lightly to coat. Add rice sticks. Toss lightly again. Makes 6 servings.

*Instead of frying rice sticks, you can substitute one 3-ounce can *chow mein noodles,* and omit the shortening or cooking oil.

Fennel-Chicken Salad

Looking for a great way to use up leftover chicken or turkey? Marinate it in wine vinegar, fennel, and rosemary for a sensational flavor.

⅓ cup olive oil *or* salad oil
¼ cup white wine vinegar
¼ teaspoon fennel seed, crushed
¼ teaspoon dried rosemary, crushed
Several drops bottled hot pepper sauce
2½ cups cubed cooked chicken *or* turkey
1½ cups sliced cauliflower *or* broccoli flowerets
3 medium plums, pitted and sliced, *or* one 8½-ounce can whole unpitted purple plums, drained, pitted, and sliced
½ cup sliced radishes
4 cups shredded Chinese cabbage
¾ cup cashews

● In a medium salad bowl combine oil, wine vinegar, fennel, rosemary, hot pepper sauce, and ¼ teaspoon *salt*. Add chicken or turkey, cauliflower or broccoli, plums, and radishes. Toss lightly to coat. Cover and chill for 2 hours.

● To serve, stir mixture in bowl. Add the Chinese cabbage and cashews. Toss lightly to mix. Makes 6 servings.

Lemony Chicken-and-Broccoli Salad

For a light and refreshing look, use only the white meat from the chicken.

¾ pound broccoli
12 ounces cooked chicken, cut into julienne strips (about 2½ cups)
1½ cups sliced fresh mushrooms
½ cup mayonnaise *or* salad dressing
½ cup plain yogurt
1 tablespoon milk
¼ teaspoon finely shredded lemon peel
Dash salt
Dash pepper
Dash Worcestershire sauce
Milk
¼ cup toasted pine nuts *or* sliced almonds, toasted
Romaine leaves

● Remove outer leaves and tough parts of stalks from the broccoli. Cut the broccoli stalks crosswise into ¼-inch-thick slices, then break the flowerets into smaller pieces. (You should have about 4 cups total.)

● In a medium covered saucepan cook broccoli in a small amount of lightly salted boiling water for 4 to 5 minutes or till nearly tender, then drain. Rinse with cold water. Drain again. In a mixing bowl combine the broccoli, chicken, and mushrooms.

● For dressing, in a small mixing bowl combine mayonnaise or salad dressing, yogurt, 1 tablespoon milk, lemon peel, salt, pepper, and Worcestershire sauce. Stir till well blended. Pour the dressing over broccoli mixture and toss lightly to coat. Cover and chill the mixture for 4 to 6 hours.

● To serve, if necessary, stir in a few tablespoons of additional milk to moisten mixture. Add nuts and toss lightly to mix. Line a medium salad bowl with lettuce leaves. Transfer the broccoli mixture to the bowl. Makes 4 servings.

Slim Chicken Slaw

You can make this low-calorie salad up to 6 hours before serving.

1 tablespoon all-purpose flour
1 tablespoon sugar
½ teaspoon salt
½ teaspoon dry mustard
½ teaspoon celery seed
½ cup skim milk
1 slightly beaten egg yolk
1 tablespoon vinegar
1 tablespoon lemon juice
3 cups shredded cabbage
2 cups chopped cooked chicken breast *or* turkey breast
1 cup seedless red grapes, halved
½ cup sliced celery
½ cup chopped walnuts

● For dressing, in a small saucepan combine flour, sugar, salt, dry mustard, and celery seed. Gradually stir in milk. Cook and stir over medium heat till thickened and bubbly. Stir *half* of the hot mixture into the beaten egg yolk, then return all to saucepan. Cook and stir over low heat for 1 to 2 minutes more or till thickened. Stir in vinegar and lemon juice, then cool mixture.

● In a medium salad bowl combine cabbage, chicken or turkey, grapes, celery, and walnuts. Pour cooled dressing over cabbage mixture and toss lightly to coat. Cover and chill for 2 to 6 hours. Makes 4 servings.

Wilted Lettuce with Chicken

"It's more than just a wilted salad," commented one of the editors on the taste panel. Chicken, apples, and mushrooms turn this lettuce salad into a hearty meal.

3 cups torn romaine
3 cups torn red leaf lettuce
1 cup sliced fresh mushrooms
¼ cup sliced green onion
1 tablespoon olive oil *or* cooking oil
1 whole large chicken breast (1 pound), skinned, boned, and cut into bite-size julienne strips
1 teaspoon mustard seed
3 tablespoons olive oil *or* cooking oil
2 tablespoons white wine vinegar
2 small apples, cut into very thin wedges
3 hard-cooked eggs, cut into wedges

● In a large mixing bowl combine romaine, leaf lettuce, mushrooms, and onion. Toss lightly to mix. Set lettuce mixture aside.

● In a 12-inch skillet heat the 1 tablespoon oil over medium-high heat. Add chicken and mustard seed, then cook and stir for 2 to 3 minutes or till chicken is tender. Reduce heat to medium.

● Stir in the 3 tablespoons oil and vinegar. Add apples, and cook and stir for 30 seconds. Remove skillet from heat. Immediately add the lettuce mixture and carefully toss about 1 minute or till lettuce begins to wilt. Spoon the lettuce mixture onto 4 salad plates. Garnish with egg wedges. Makes 4 servings.

Wilting lettuce
After cooking the apples, remove the skillet from the heat. Immediately add the lettuce mixture to the hot dressing in the skillet. Then carefully toss the lettuce with the dressing for 1 minute or until the lettuce begins to wilt and is no longer crisp, as shown. The lettuce wilts because of the heat from the dressing and the skillet.

Spoon the mixture onto salad plates and garnish with hard-cooked egg wedges. Serve the salad while the lettuce is still warm.

Paella Salad

Our version of paella (pah-ALE-yuh) is a salad. Traditionally, paella is a Spanish rice casserole flavored with saffron.

2 cups water
1 cup long grain rice
2 teaspoons instant chicken
   bouillon granules
½ teaspoon ground red pepper
¼ teaspoon thread saffron,
   crushed, *or* ground
   turmeric
2 cups cooked chicken cut
   into julienne strips
1 8-ounce package frozen
   cooked shrimp, thawed
2 medium tomatoes, seeded
   and chopped
1 14-ounce can artichoke
   hearts, drained and cut up
1 cup frozen peas, thawed
¼ cup sliced green onion
¾ cup clear French salad
   dressing

● In a medium saucepan combine water, rice, bouillon granules, red pepper, saffron or turmeric, and ¼ teaspoon *salt*. Bring to boiling, then reduce heat. Cover with a tight-fitting lid. Cook about 15 minutes or till all water is absorbed. Remove from heat and let stand, covered, for 10 minutes.

● In a very large mixing bowl combine the warm rice, chicken, shrimp, tomatoes, artichokes, peas, and onion. Toss lightly to mix. Pour dressing over rice mixture and toss lightly to coat. Cover and chill for 4 hours or overnight. Makes 8 servings.

Scandinavian Greens

The refreshing lemon-dill dressing adds a Scandinavian touch to this salad.

3½ cups torn red leaf lettuce
2½ cups torn Bibb lettuce *or*
   Boston lettuce
1 8-ounce package frozen
   cooked shrimp, thawed
1 cup frozen peas, thawed
½ of a small cucumber, halved
   lengthwise and sliced
2 green onions, sliced
¼ cup olive oil *or* salad oil
2 tablespoons lemon juice
1 tablespoon white wine
   vinegar
1 teaspoon Dijon-style
   mustard
½ teaspoon dried dillweed
   Plain croutons *or* Dill
   Croutons (see recipe,
   page 87)

● In a very large salad bowl combine red leaf lettuce, Bibb or Boston lettuce, shrimp, peas, cucumber, and green onions. Cover and chill while preparing dressing.

● For dressing, in a screw-top jar combine oil, lemon juice, vinegar, mustard, dillweed, ¼ teaspoon *salt*, and ⅛ teaspoon *pepper*. Cover and shake well. Pour dressing over lettuce mixture. Toss lightly to coat. Top with croutons. Makes 4 servings.

Curried Seafood Salad

Curry powder is not a single spice but a blend of many spices.

¼ cup tarragon vinegar
1 tablespoon honey
1½ to 2 teaspoons curry powder
⅓ cup salad oil
5 cups torn Bibb lettuce *or*
   Boston lettuce
3 cups torn spinach
1 cup sliced celery
½ of a cucumber, sliced
1 8-ounce package frozen
   cooked shrimp, thawed
1 6-ounce package frozen
   crabmeat, thawed and
   drained
½ cup coconut, toasted
½ cup slivered almonds,
   toasted
½ cup raisins

● For dressing, in a blender container combine vinegar, honey, and curry powder. Cover and blend for 5 seconds. Through the opening in the lid or with lid ajar, and with blender on slow speed, *gradually* add oil in a thin stream. (When necessary, stop blender and scrape sides.) Cover and blend till thickened. Cover and chill dressing.

● In a very large mixing bowl combine Bibb or Boston lettuce, spinach, celery, cucumber, shrimp, and crabmeat. Pour the dressing over lettuce mixture and toss lightly to coat.

● Immediately transfer mixture to a large salad bowl. Pass coconut, almonds, and raisins to sprinkle on individual servings. Makes 6 servings.

Gazpacho Salad with Shrimp

4 medium tomatoes, each cut
   into eight wedges
1 medium cucumber, thinly
   sliced
1 8-ounce package frozen
   cooked shrimp, thawed
1 medium green pepper,
   coarsely chopped
½ cup sliced celery
⅓ cup coarsely chopped onion
3 tablespoons snipped parsley
⅓ cup red wine vinegar
¼ cup salad oil
2 cloves garlic, minced
½ teaspoon salt
¼ teaspoon ground cumin
   Few drops bottled hot
     pepper sauce
   Dash pepper
4 Bibb lettuce *or* iceberg
   lettuce cups
   Plain croutons

● In a large mixing bowl combine tomatoes, cucumber, shrimp, green pepper, celery, onion, and parsley.

● For dressing, in a screw-top jar combine vinegar, oil, garlic, salt, cumin, hot pepper sauce, and pepper. Cover and shake well. Pour over tomato mixture and toss lightly to coat. Cover and chill for 2 to 3 hours, lightly tossing mixture occasionally.

● To serve, using a slotted spoon to drain, spoon tomato mixture into lettuce cups. Top with croutons. Makes 4 servings.

Curried Seafood Salad

Sweet-and-Sour Pasta Salad

To keep the broccoli bright green and the nuts crunchy, add them just before serving.

1 tablespoon cornstarch
1 tablespoon brown sugar
½ teaspoon ground ginger
¼ teaspoon garlic powder
1 6-ounce can unsweetened
    pineapple juice
¼ cup white wine vinegar
2 tablespoons water
2 tablespoons soy sauce
1½ cups broccoli flowerets
2 cups pasta bow ties
1 8-ounce package frozen
    cooked shrimp, thawed
1 medium carrot, thinly bias
    sliced
½ cup peanuts *or* cashews

● For dressing, in a small saucepan combine cornstarch, sugar, ginger, and garlic powder. Stir in juice, vinegar, water, and soy sauce. Cook and stir till thickened and bubbly. Cook and stir for 2 minutes more. Remove from heat and cool.

● Meanwhile, in a medium covered saucepan cook broccoli in a small amount of lightly salted boiling water for 4 to 5 minutes or till nearly tender, then drain. Rinse with cold water, then drain again. Cover and chill.

● In another saucepan cook pasta according to package directions, then drain. Rinse with cold water, then drain again.

● In a medium salad bowl combine pasta, shrimp, and carrot. Pour dressing over pasta mixture and toss lightly to coat. Cover and chill for 2 to 8 hours, lightly tossing mixture occasionally.

● To serve, add chilled broccoli and peanuts or cashews. Toss lightly to mix. Makes 4 servings.

Crab and Kiwi-Fruit Salads

Company coming? Here's an easy but elegant idea. Just serve with a few sesame toast crackers and iced tea, and you've got a complete meal.

⅔ cup mayonnaise *or* salad
    dressing
2 tablespoons thinly sliced
    green onion
2 teaspoons lemon juice
½ teaspoon ground ginger
    Dash ground red pepper
2 8-ounce packages frozen
    salad-style crab-flavored
    fish, thawed
4 kiwi fruits, peeled and sliced
    crosswise
¼ cup sliced almonds, toasted

● In a medium mixing bowl combine mayonnaise or salad dressing, green onion, lemon juice, ginger, and red pepper. Stir till well blended.

● Fold crab-flavored fish into mayonnaise mixture. If desired, cover and chill for up to 6 hours.

● For salads, overlap kiwi slices around the outer edges of 4 salad plates. Spoon crab mixture onto centers of plates. Sprinkle with almonds. Makes 4 servings.

Avocado and Seafood Salad

The crab-flavored fish sticks are sometimes called surimi. This "seafood" is actually a blend of whitefish and crabmeat.

½ cup dairy sour cream
2 tablespoons frozen orange juice concentrate, thawed
1 to 2 tablespoons milk
2 8-ounce packages frozen crab-flavored fish sticks, thawed and cut into 1-inch pieces
3 cups torn Bibb lettuce *or* Boston lettuce
1 cup torn escarole
1 11-ounce can mandarin orange sections, drained
¼ cup sliced almonds, toasted
1 avocado, seeded, peeled, and sliced crosswise

● For dressing, in a mixing bowl combine sour cream and orange juice concentrate. Stir till well blended. Stir in enough milk to make dressing of desired consistency. Cover and chill.

● For salad, in a large salad bowl combine fish pieces, lettuce, escarole, orange sections, and almonds. Add avocado slices. Pour dressing over lettuce mixture and toss lightly to coat. Makes 4 servings.

Preparing an avocado

To remove the seed from an avocado, cut the fruit lengthwise around the seed. Then, with your hands, gently twist the halves in opposite directions to separate.

Carefully tap the seed with the cutting edge of a sharp knife so the blade is caught in the seed. Rotate the knife to loosen the seed, then use the knife to lift the seed out, as shown.

To peel the avocado, place it cut side down in your palm. Use the sharp knife to loosen and strip the skin from the fruit.

Tuna and Pasta Salad

Our Test Kitchen also suggests serving this colorful salad in a lettuce-lined bowl.

2 cups tiny shell macaroni
1 12½-ounce can tuna, drained and flaked
½ cup shredded Swiss cheese
½ cup shredded cheddar cheese
1 stalk celery, sliced
¼ cup sliced green onion
½ cup mayonnaise *or* salad dressing
½ cup plain yogurt
1 tablespoon milk
½ teaspoon garlic salt
½ teaspoon dried dillweed
   Milk
1 medium tomato, seeded and cut into thin strips
   Bibb lettuce *or* Boston lettuce leaves
   Lemon *or* lime wedges

● Cook shell macaroni according to package directions, then drain. Rinse with cold water, then drain again.

● In a medium mixing bowl combine pasta, tuna, Swiss cheese, cheddar cheese, celery, and green onion.

● For dressing, in a small mixing bowl combine the mayonnaise or salad dressing, yogurt, 1 tablespoon milk, garlic salt, and dillweed. Stir till well blended. Pour dressing over pasta mixture and toss lightly to coat. Cover and chill for 2 to 8 hours.

● To serve, if necessary, stir in a few tablespoons of additional milk to moisten mixture. Add tomato and toss lightly. Line 6 salad plates with lettuce. Spoon pasta mixture onto the plates. Garnish with lemon or lime wedges. Makes 6 servings.

Tossed Salade Niçoise

Pronounced sah-LAHD nee-SWAHZ, this Mediterranean salad makes either 12 appetizer or 6 to 8 main-dish servings.

2 medium potatoes, peeled and sliced ¼ inch thick
1 9-ounce package frozen cut green beans
1 cup cherry tomatoes, halved
1 small green pepper, seeded and cut into strips
¼ cup sliced pitted ripe olives
¾ cup clear Italian salad dressing
4 cups torn romaine
3 cups torn Bibb lettuce *or* Boston lettuce
1 9¼-ounce can water-packed tuna, drained, flaked, and chilled
2 hard-cooked eggs, sliced
1 2-ounce can anchovy fillets, drained

● In a medium covered saucepan cook potatoes in lightly salted boiling water for 5 minutes. Break up the frozen beans and add them to the potatoes in the saucepan. Return to boiling. Cover and boil gently for 4 to 6 minutes more or till nearly tender, then drain. Cool vegetables slightly.

● In a very large salad bowl combine potatoes, green beans, tomatoes, green pepper, and olives. Pour dressing over vegetables. Toss lightly to coat. Cover and chill for 2 to 3 hours.

● To serve, add romaine, Bibb or Boston lettuce, and tuna. Toss lightly to coat. Garnish with egg slices and anchovy fillets. Makes 6 to 8 servings.

Tuna-Orange Toss

Here's a tip for a prettier salad: Use the solid white tuna because it breaks up less when the salad is tossed.

1½ teaspoons cornstarch
1½ teaspoons sugar
¼ teaspoon dry mustard
¼ teaspoon paprika
⅛ teaspoon salt
   Dash pepper
½ cup orange juice
2 tablespoons catsup
1 tablespoon salad oil
4 cups torn iceberg lettuce
1 11-ounce can mandarin
   orange sections, drained
½ of a small cucumber, sliced
⅓ cup sliced radishes
1 9¼-ounce can water-packed
   tuna, drained, broken into
   chunks, and chilled

● For dressing, in a small saucepan combine cornstarch, sugar, dry mustard, paprika, salt, and pepper. Stir in orange juice. Cook and stir till thickened and bubbly. Cook and stir for 2 minutes more. Remove from heat. Stir in the catsup and salad oil. Cover and chill.

● For salad, in a medium salad bowl combine lettuce, orange sections, cucumber, and radishes. Stir dressing and pour over mixture. Toss to coat. Add tuna and toss lightly. Serves 4.

Cod-Spinach Salad with Lemon-Mustard Dressing

Try a vegetable peeler instead of a knife to easily cut strips of peel from the lemon.

1½ pounds fresh *or* frozen cod
   fillets
¼ cup dry white wine
¼ cup water
1 egg
1 large clove garlic, quartered
2 1x½-inch strips lemon peel
3 tablespoons lemon juice
1 tablespoon Dijon-style
   mustard
½ teaspoon dried thyme,
   crushed
¼ teaspoon sugar
1 cup olive oil *or* salad oil
1 to 3 tablespoons milk
5 cups torn spinach
5 cups torn sorrel*
1½ cups sliced fresh
   mushrooms
½ cup sliced radishes
   Snipped chives

● Thaw fish, if frozen. Cut fish into 1-inch cubes. Place fish in a large skillet. Add wine, water, and ¼ teaspoon *salt*. Bring to boiling, then reduce heat. Cover and simmer for 3 to 6 minutes or till fish flakes easily with a fork. Drain and cool the fish slightly, then chill.

● For dressing, in a blender container or food processor bowl combine egg, garlic, lemon peel, lemon juice, mustard, thyme, sugar, ¼ teaspoon *salt*, and ⅛ teaspoon *pepper*. Cover and blend or process till smooth. Through the opening in the lid or with lid ajar, and with blender or food processor on slow speed, *gradually* add oil in a thin stream. (When necessary, stop blender and scrape sides.) Cover and blend about 20 seconds more or till thickened. If necessary, stir in enough milk to make dressing of desired consistency. Cover and chill.

● To serve, in a very large mixing bowl combine fish, spinach, sorrel, mushrooms, and radishes. Toss lightly to mix. Spoon spinach mixture onto 6 salad plates. Drizzle with dressing and sprinkle with chives. Makes 6 servings.

*If sorrel is unavailable, substitute additional spinach.

Minted Pea-and-Fish Salad

To substitute a fresh herb for the dried form, use three times more of the fresh.

1 pound fresh *or* frozen fish
 fillets
¼ cup dry white wine
2 cups fresh peas *or* one
 10-ounce package frozen
 peas
1 teaspoon sugar
1 teaspoon dried mint,
 crushed
¼ teaspoon dried rosemary,
 crushed
½ cup mayonnaise *or* salad
 dressing
2 tablespoons lemon yogurt
2 tablespoons milk
 Several dashes bottled hot
 pepper sauce
½ cup thinly sliced celery
½ cup sliced fresh mushrooms
4 Bibb *or* Boston lettuce cups

● Thaw fish, if frozen. Cut into 1-inch cubes. Place fish in a large skillet. Add wine, ¼ cup *water*, and ¼ teaspoon *salt*. Bring to boiling, then reduce the heat. Cover and simmer for 3 to 6 minutes or till fish flakes easily with a fork. Drain. Cool fish slightly, then cover and chill.

● Meanwhile, in a small saucepan combine peas, sugar, mint, rosemary, ½ cup *water*, and ¼ teaspoon *salt*. Cover and cook till peas are nearly tender, adding more water if necessary (allow about 5 minutes for frozen or 10 to 12 minutes for fresh). Drain. Cool slightly, then cover and chill.

● For dressing, in a small bowl combine mayonnaise or salad dressing, yogurt, milk, and hot pepper sauce. Stir till well blended. Cover and chill.

● To serve, in a medium mixing bowl combine chilled fish, peas, celery, and mushrooms. Toss lightly to mix. Spoon pea mixture into lettuce cups. Drizzle with dressing. If desired, garnish with radish roses or tomato wedges. Makes 4 servings.

Salmon and Melon Salad

2 fresh *or* frozen salmon
 steaks, cut ¾ to 1 inch
 thick (about 1 pound
 total)
¾ cup water
1 tablespoon thinly sliced
 green onion
1 bay leaf
½ of a 5-ounce can (⅓ cup)
 evaporated milk
½ of a 6-ounce can (⅓ cup)
 frozen orange juice
 concentrate, thawed
3 teaspoons salad oil
½ of a medium cantaloupe,
 seeded
½ of a medium honeydew
 melon, seeded and peeled
2 cups torn Bibb lettuce *or*
 Boston lettuce
1½ cups seedless red grapes

● Thaw salmon, if frozen. In a skillet combine water, green onion, bay leaf, ¼ teaspoon *salt,* and dash *pepper.* Bring to boiling, then add salmon. Reduce heat. Cover and simmer for 5 to 10 minutes or till fish flakes easily with a fork. Drain and cool slightly. Remove skin and bones. Break salmon into large pieces. Cover and chill.

● For dressing, in a blender container combine evaporated milk and orange juice concentrate. Cover and blend about 5 seconds or till well combined. With lid ajar and blender on slow speed, *gradually* add oil, 1 teaspoon at a time. (When necessary, stop blender and scrape sides.) Cover and chill.

● Using a melon-ball cutter, scoop pulp out of the cantaloupe. Using a crinkle-edge cutter or a knife, cut the honeydew melon into ¾-inch cubes. (You should have about 1½ cups *each* of the cantaloupe balls and the honeydew melon cubes.)

● For salad, combine cantaloupe, honeydew melon, lettuce, and grapes. Pour dressing over mixture. Toss lightly. Add salmon and toss lightly again. Spoon mixture into 4 bowls. Serves 4.

Salmon and Melon Salad

Bulgur Salad in a Pocket

Here's one for all you nut lovers. Peanuts, bulgur, and wheat germ give this hearty sandwich a delicious flavor.

1 cup boiling water
2 teaspoons instant chicken bouillon granules
½ cup bulgur wheat
1 8-ounce carton plain yogurt
¼ cup mayonnaise *or* salad dressing
¼ teaspoon curry powder
1 small apple, cored and chopped
½ cup coarsely chopped peanuts
½ cup wheat germ
⅓ cup sliced celery
⅓ cup raisins
4 large pita bread rounds, halved crosswise
  Leaf lettuce

● In a medium mixing bowl combine boiling water and chicken bouillon granules, stirring till granules are dissolved. Stir in bulgur and let stand for 20 minutes. Drain well, then squeeze out excess liquid. Set bulgur aside.

● In a medium mixing bowl combine yogurt, mayonnaise or salad dressing, and curry powder. Stir till well blended. Add the drained bulgur, apple, peanuts, wheat germ, celery, and raisins. Toss lightly to coat. Cover and chill for 1 to 2 hours.

● To serve, line the insides of pita halves with lettuce leaves. Spoon bulgur mixture into the pita halves. Makes 4 servings.

Egg-Chard Toss

You'll find Swiss chard packs more of a bite than spinach.

1 8-ounce carton plain yogurt
2 to 3 teaspoons prepared horseradish
1 teaspoon sugar
½ teaspoon salt
  Dash bottled hot pepper sauce
  Milk
4 cups torn spinach
4 cups torn Swiss chard*
4 ounces cheddar cheese, cut into 1-inch julienne sticks
1 cup cherry tomatoes, halved
¼ cup sliced green onion
4 hard-cooked eggs, sliced

● For dressing, in a small mixing bowl combine yogurt, horseradish, sugar, salt, and hot pepper sauce. Stir till well blended. If necessary, stir in enough milk to make dressing of desired consistency. Cover and chill dressing while preparing the salad.

● For salad, in a large salad bowl combine spinach, Swiss chard, cheddar cheese, tomatoes, and onion. Toss lightly to mix. Add eggs. Pour dressing over spinach mixture. Toss lightly to coat. Makes 6 servings.

*If Swiss chard is unavailable, substitute additional spinach.

Tortellini and Parsley-Pesto Salad

1 cup lightly packed parsley sprigs with stems removed

2 teaspoons dried basil, crushed

1 clove garlic

⅓ cup grated Parmesan cheese *or* Romano cheese

¼ cup olive oil *or* salad oil

8 ounces broccoli

2 7-ounce packages cheese-filled tortellini

1 2¼-ounce can sliced pitted ripe olives, drained

6 ounces provolone cheese *or* mozzarella cheese, cubed

2 medium tomatoes, seeded and chopped

⅓ cup pine nuts, toasted, *or* ½ cup broken walnuts

● For pesto, in a food processor bowl or blender container combine parsley, basil, and garlic. Cover and process or blend till finely chopped. (When necessary, stop and scrape sides.) Add Parmesan or Romano cheese. Cover and process or blend till combined. With lid ajar, add oil a little at a time, processing or blending after each addition till well combined. Set pesto aside.

● Remove outer leaves and tough parts of stalks from broccoli. Cut the stalks crosswise into ¼-inch-thick slices, then break flowerets into smaller pieces. (You should have about 2½ cups total.) Set broccoli aside.

● In a large covered saucepan cook the tortellini according to package directions, adding the broccoli during the last 5 minutes of cooking. Drain.

● In a large salad bowl combine pesto, broccoli, tortellini, and olives. Toss lightly. Cover and chill for 4 hours or overnight.

● To serve, add provolone or mozzarella cheese, tomatoes, and nuts to the tortellini mixture. Toss lightly to mix. Serves 6.

Making parsley pesto

Pesto means "pounding" in Italian. Traditionally this sauce is made with a mortar and pestle. To simplify the method, use a food processor or a blender.

Start with about 1¼ ounces of parsley sprigs. Remove and discard the stems. (You should have 1 cup of loosely packed parsley.) Place the parsley, basil, and garlic in a food processor bowl or a blender container. Cover and process or blend till finely chopped. If necessary, stop the processor or blender and scrape the parsley mixture from the sides of the container. This first step of processing is important to assure a smooth pesto.

Cheesy Apple Salad

You'll find Edam (EED-um) and Gouda (GOO-duh) cheese have a mild and nutty flavor.

3 tablespoons mayonnaise *or* salad dressing
3 tablespoons plain yogurt
1 teaspoon honey
¼ teaspoon celery seed
2 cups torn iceberg lettuce *or* spinach
2 small apples, cored and coarsely chopped
4 ounces Edam cheese *or* Gouda cheese, cubed
1 stalk celery, sliced
¼ cup broken walnuts

● For dressing, in a small mixing bowl combine mayonnaise or salad dressing, yogurt, honey, and celery seed. Stir till well blended. Cover and chill.

● In a large mixing bowl combine lettuce or spinach, apples, cheese, celery, and *half* of the walnuts. Pour the dressing over lettuce mixture and toss lightly to coat.

● Immediately spoon the lettuce mixture onto 2 salad plates. Sprinkle with the remaining walnuts. Makes 2 servings.

Three-Bean and Cheese Salad

Here's a south-of-the-border serving idea: Spoon this creamy bean mixture into the crispy tortilla shells from the Taco Salads on page 67.

⅓ cup creamy buttermilk salad dressing
2 green onions, thinly sliced
¼ teaspoon dried basil, crushed
1 8½-ounce can lima beans, drained, *or* ⅔ cup frozen lima beans, cooked and drained
1 8-ounce can red kidney beans, drained
1 cup drained canned garbanzo beans
6 ounces Monterey Jack, cheddar, *or* Swiss cheese, cut into 2-inch julienne sticks
1 cup thinly bias-sliced carrots
½ cup sliced celery
Milk
Red leaf lettuce

● In a medium mixing bowl combine the salad dressing, green onions, and basil. Stir till well blended.

● Add beans, cheese, carrots, and celery. Toss lightly to coat. Cover and chill for 2 hours or overnight.

● To serve, if necessary, stir in a few tablespoons of milk to moisten bean mixture. Line a medium serving platter with lettuce leaves. Mound the bean mixture onto the platter. Serves 4.

ARRANGED OR LAYERED

Make
Layered Fiesta Salad
the night before or
arrange Gingered Shrimp
Salads right before serving.
Either way, each recipe in
this chapter is guaranteed
to produce eye-catching
and delicious results.

Salad-Making Hints

Easy-to-Make Garnishes

Here are seven elegant garnishes that take only minutes to make. What's more, they can be made ahead. Just store them in ice water until you're ready to use them.

● *Radish Roses:* Cut off the root tip of each radish. Then make four or five petals by cutting thin slices from the top to, *but not through,* the bottom of each radish. Leave a little red between each of the petals. Chill the radishes in ice water until the petals open.

● *Carrot Curls* or *Zigzags:* With a vegetable peeler, cut thin lengthwise strips from a carrot. For curls, roll up each strip and secure it with a wooden toothpick. For zigzags, thread each strip, accordion-style, on a toothpick. Then place them in ice water to crisp.

● *Citrus Twists:* Thinly slice lemons, limes, or oranges. Then make a cut from the edge to the center of each slice. Twist the ends in opposite directions.

● *Scored Cucumber Slices:* Run the tines of a fork down the length of a cucumber, pressing to break through the peel. Repeat at regular intervals. Then slice the cucumber.

● *Celery* or *Green Onion Brushes:* Trim the ends from celery stalks or green onions. Cut the celery into 4-inch pieces. At one or both ends of each vegetable, cut about six lengthwise slits about 2 inches long. Place the vegetables in ice water till slits open.

Serving Containers

Need to choose which bowl, plate, or platter to serve your salad on? Consider the size, color, and pattern of the bowl or plate.

For example, be sure a tossed salad doesn't fill the bowl to its rim. Otherwise, you won't have room for mixing. For layered salads, we recommend using a clear glass bowl. Glass lets you see the pretty layers.

For an arranged salad, choose a plate or platter with a simple pattern and one that's not too colorful. You'll want the plate to complement the salad, not overwhelm it.

Beef and Vegetable Plates

Turn leftover steak into a fresh-tasting, new meal.

¼ cup finely chopped spinach
1 egg yolk
1 tablespoon tarragon vinegar
¼ teaspoon salt
⅛ teaspoon dry mustard
½ cup salad oil
3 to 4 tablespoons milk
12 ounces asparagus
1 pound baby carrots
  Bibb lettuce *or* Boston
    lettuce leaves
8 ounces thinly sliced cooked
    beef, cut into julienne
    strips (about 1½ cups)
3 medium tomatoes, cut into
    wedges
1 small onion, sliced and
    separated into rings

● For dressing, in a blender container combine spinach, egg yolk, tarragon vinegar, salt, and dry mustard. Cover and blend for 10 seconds. Through the opening in the lid or with the lid ajar, and with blender on slow speed, *gradually* add oil in a thin stream. (When necessary, stop the blender and scrape the sides.) Stir in enough of the milk to make dressing of desired consistency. Cover and chill.

● Meanwhile, cut woody base from asparagus. Scrape off scales, then cut spears in half.

● In a large covered saucepan cook carrots in a small amount of lightly salted boiling water for 10 minutes. Add asparagus pieces and continue cooking for 5 to 10 minutes more or till the vegetables are nearly tender, then drain. Rinse with cold water, then drain again. Cover and chill.

● For salads, line 4 salad plates with lettuce leaves. Arrange asparagus, carrots, beef, and tomato wedges in separate piles on the plates, filling surfaces of plates. Top with onion rings. Serve dressing separately. Makes 4 servings.

Beef with Basil Dressing

The rounded edges of the tomato slices and cucumbers form a petallike design.

⅓ cup olive oil *or* salad oil
¼ cup lemon juice
3 tablespoons dry sherry
12 ounces thinly sliced cooked
    beef, cut into julienne
    strips (about 2½ cups)
½ cup thinly sliced green
    onion
½ cup mayonnaise *or* salad
    dressing
1 tablespoon snipped fresh
    basil *or* 1 teaspoon dried
    basil, crushed
2 small tomatoes, halved and
    thinly sliced
1 medium cucumber, thinly
    sliced
2 cups sliced fresh
    mushrooms

● In a medium bowl combine oil, lemon juice, sherry, and ½ teaspoon *salt*. Add beef and onion. Toss lightly to coat. Let stand at room temperature for 20 minutes. Drain beef-onion mixture, reserving 3 tablespoons of the liquid.

● For dressing, in a small mixing bowl combine mayonnaise or salad dressing, basil, and reserved liquid. Stir till well blended.

● For salads, around the outer edges of 4 salad plates, alternately overlap tomato and cucumber slices. (Place rounded edges of tomatoes toward the outer edges of the plates, forming petallike shapes.) Near inner edges of the tomato-cucumber rings, place rings of mushroom slices. Spoon beef mixture into centers of plates. If desired, garnish with fresh basil leaves. Serve dressing separately. Makes 4 servings.

Layered Fiesta Salad

1   15-ounce can garbanzo
    beans, drained
5   cups shredded iceberg
    lettuce *or* torn romaine
2   cups chopped cooked beef
1   medium tomato, seeded and
    chopped
¼   cup sliced pitted ripe olives
¼   cup sliced celery
¼   cup sliced green onion
¾   cup shredded cheddar
    cheese
1   8-ounce carton dairy sour
    cream
1   6-ounce container frozen
    avocado dip, thawed
½   cup milk
½   teaspoon sugar
½   teaspoon chili powder
¼   teaspoon salt
2   tablespoons chopped
    canned green chili
    peppers
1   clove garlic, minced
2   slices bacon, crisp-cooked,
    drained, and crumbled
1   cup crushed tortilla chips

● In a large clear glass salad bowl layer garbanzo beans, lettuce, beef, tomato, olives, celery, onion, and cheese.

● For dressing, in a small mixing bowl combine the sour cream, avocado dip, milk, sugar, chili powder, and salt. Stir till well blended. Stir in green chili peppers and garlic. Spread dressing over top of salad. Cover and chill for up to 24 hours.

● To serve, top with the crumbled bacon. Then sprinkle with tortilla chips. Makes 6 to 8 servings.

Pork and Papaya Salads

¼   cup dried currants
½   cup white wine vinegar
¼   cup walnut oil *or* salad oil
¼   cup chicken broth
1   tablespoon honey
¼   teaspoon ground cinnamon
1   pound cooked boneless pork
    loin roast
1   head Belgian endive
    Bibb lettuce leaves
2   papayas, seeded, peeled, and
    sliced lengthwise
2   avocados, seeded, peeled,
    and sliced lengthwise
¼   cup broken walnuts

● In a small bowl pour enough boiling *water* over currants to cover. Let stand for 5 minutes, then drain.

● For dressing, in a screw-top jar combine vinegar, oil, chicken broth, honey, and cinnamon. Cover and shake well.

● For salads, trim fat from pork roast and slice thinly. Separate leaves of Belgian endive. Line 6 salad plates with Bibb lettuce leaves. Arrange pork, Belgian endive, papaya, and avocado on the plates. Sprinkle with currants and walnuts. Drizzle the dressing evenly over salads. If desired, garnish with julienne strips of lime peel. Makes 6 servings.

Pork and Papaya Salads

Prosciutto and Fruit Salads

Make-ahead tip: Assemble, cover, and chill these salads up to four hours in advance. Then add the peaches, dressing, and nuts right before serving.

¼ cup whipping cream
½ cup mayonnaise *or* salad dressing
¼ cup crumbled blue cheese
1 tablespoon milk
½ of a medium cantaloupe, seeded
½ of a medium honeydew melon, seeded
  Leaf lettuce
8 ounces thinly sliced prosciutto *or* fully cooked ham
1 large peach, peeled, pitted, and sliced, *or* nectarine, pitted and sliced
1 cup strawberries, halved
2 tablespoons coarsely chopped pistachio nuts

● For dressing, in a small mixing bowl whip the cream till soft peaks form. Fold in mayonnaise or salad dressing and blue cheese. If necessary, stir in milk to make dressing of desired consistency. Cover and chill while preparing other ingredients.

● Using a melon-ball cutter, scoop pulp out of the cantaloupe and honeydew melon.

● For salads, line 4 salad plates with lettuce leaves. Roll up each slice of meat jelly-roll style. Arrange the rolled meat slices on one side of each plate. On the other side of each plate, arrange cantaloupe and honeydew melon balls, peach or nectarine slices, and strawberries. Spoon dressing over top of each salad. Sprinkle with pistachio nuts. Makes 4 servings.

Chicken-Orange Salads

You can use fresh pea pods instead of the frozen if you cook them first.

¼ cup salad oil
1 tablespoon finely shredded orange peel
¼ cup orange juice
1 tablespoon honey
1 tablespoon dry sherry
¼ teaspoon garlic salt
⅛ teaspoon white pepper
3 cups cubed cooked chicken *or* turkey
1 green onion, thinly sliced
1 cup sliced fresh mushrooms
½ of a 6-ounce package (about 1 cup) frozen pea pods, thawed
8 thin orange slices, halved

● For dressing, in a screw-top jar combine salad oil, orange peel, orange juice, honey, sherry, garlic salt, and white pepper. Cover and shake well. In a medium mixing bowl pour dressing over chicken or turkey and onion. Toss lightly to coat. Cover and chill for 6 hours or overnight, stirring mixture occasionally.

● For salads, add mushrooms to chicken mixture. Toss lightly to coat. At the tops of 4 salad plates arrange pea pods in fan shapes. Spoon chicken mixture onto the centers of the plates, next to the pea pods. Then next to the chicken mixture, at the bottoms of the plates, overlap the orange slices. Serves 4.

Chicken Salad on Melon

Melon, strawberries, and poppy seed dressing spell S-C-R-U-M-P-T-I-O-U-S-!

2 tablespoons sugar
2 tablespoons vinegar
1 tablespoon lemon juice
⅛ teaspoon dry mustard
    Dash salt
¼ cup salad oil
¼ teaspoon poppy seed
1½ cups cubed cooked chicken
    or turkey
¼ of a medium cantaloupe
¼ of a medium honeydew
    melon
2 Bibb lettuce *or* Boston
    lettuce cups
1 cup strawberries, quartered
½ cup walnut halves
    Whole strawberries

● For dressing, in a blender container combine sugar, vinegar, lemon juice, dry mustard, and salt. Cover and blend for 5 seconds. Through the opening in the lid or with lid ajar, and with the blender on slow speed, *gradually* add oil in a thin stream. (When necessary, stop blender and scrape sides.) Cover and blend for 1 to 2 minutes more or till the dressing is slightly thickened. Stir in poppy seed.

● In a medium mixing bowl pour the dressing over chicken or turkey. Toss lightly to coat. Cover and chill for 30 to 45 minutes.

● Meanwhile, remove seeds from cantaloupe and honeydew melon. Peel melons and slice pulp lengthwise into ¼-inch-thick slices. Cover and chill.

● For salads, place lettuce cups in centers of 2 salad plates. Alternately overlap cantaloupe and honeydew melon slices around the lettuce cups, forming rings. Add 1 cup strawberries and walnuts to chicken mixture, then toss lightly to coat. Spoon chicken mixture into lettuce cups. Garnish with the whole strawberries. Makes 2 servings.

Gourmet's Delight

Look for the smoked turkey breast at the deli.

½ cup peach yogurt
1 3-ounce package cream
    cheese, softened
4 medium peaches, pears, *or*
    nectarines; *or* 8 small
    apricots; *or* 4 kiwi fruits
    Bibb lettuce *or* Boston
    lettuce leaves
12 ounces fully cooked smoked
    turkey breast, turkey
    roast, *or* ham, sliced
¼ cup chopped macadamia
    nuts, pistachio nuts,
    or cashews

● For dressing, in a small mixer bowl combine yogurt and cream cheese. Beat with an electric mixer on medium speed till well blended. Cover and chill.

● If necessary, peel the fruit. Then slice it.

● For salads, line 4 salad plates with lettuce leaves. From the tops to the bottoms of the plates, overlap slices of turkey or ham. Then slightly overlap fruit slices on meat. Spoon dressing over top of each salad. Sprinkle with nuts. Makes 4 servings.

Lots-of-Layers Picnic Salad

Lots-of-Layers Picnic Salad

What's your fancy for salad dressing—toasted onion, cucumber, blue cheese, or chive? You choose the flavor.

4   cups torn mixed greens
2½ cups chopped cooked
    chicken
2   small tomatoes, cut into
    thin wedges
1   10-ounce package frozen
    whole kernel corn *or* peas,
    thawed
¼   cup chopped red onion
1½ cups sliced celery
1   cup mayonnaise *or* salad
    dressing
1   8-ounce carton desired
    sour cream dip
1   8-ounce package finely
    shredded cheddar cheese
½   cup sliced radishes

● In a large clear glass salad bowl layer the torn mixed greens, chicken, tomatoes, corn or peas, red onion, and celery.

● For dressing, in a small mixing bowl combine mayonnaise or salad dressing and sour cream dip. Stir till well blended. Spread dressing over top of salad. Cover and chill for up to 24 hours.

● To serve, sprinkle with cheese and garnish with radish slices. Makes 10 to 12 servings.

Rice Stick and Shrimp Salads

Look for miso, a soybean paste, at an Oriental store. It'll add zest to the dressing.

1   12-ounce package frozen
    peeled and deveined
    shrimp
    Shortening *or* cooking oil for
    deep-fat frying
1½ ounces rice sticks
½   cup salad oil
¼   cup rice wine vinegar *or*
    cider vinegar
2   tablespoons miso paste *or*
    soy sauce
1   teaspoon honey
¼   teaspoon five-spice powder
1   medium zucchini *or* yellow
    summer squash
5   ounces jicama *or* one
    8-ounce can sliced
    water chestnuts, drained
3   cups torn spinach
1   6-ounce package frozen
    pea pods, thawed
½   cup sliced radishes

● Cook shrimp according to package directions, then drain. Rinse with cold water, then drain again and chill.

● Meanwhile, in a 3-quart saucepan or a deep-fat fryer heat 2 inches of shortening or cooking oil to 375°. Fry *unsoaked* rice sticks, a few at a time, about 5 seconds or just till sticks puff and rise to the top. Drain on paper towels. Set rice sticks aside. (You should have about 6 cups.)

● For dressing, in a screw-top jar combine salad oil, vinegar, miso paste or soy sauce, honey, five-spice powder, and ¼ cup *water*. Cover and shake well.

● Just before assembling the salads, cut the shrimp lengthwise in half. Cut the zucchini or yellow squash lengthwise in half, then slice. If using jicama, peel and cut it into 2-inch julienne sticks. (You should have about 1 cup.)

● For salads, arrange spinach on 6 salad plates. Place rice sticks in the centers of the plates. Arrange shrimp, zucchini or yellow squash, jicama or water chestnuts, pea pods, and radishes around the outer edges. Serve dressing separately. Serves 6.

Spring Greens Salads

Don't wait till spring to sink your teeth into this salad. Use romaine or leaf lettuce when sorrel is unavailable.

⅔ cup mayonnaise *or* salad dressing
½ cup crumbled blue cheese
1 tablespoon milk
1 tablespoon lemon juice
Few drops bottled hot pepper sauce
4 cups shredded iceberg lettuce
2 cups torn sorrel, romaine, *or* red leaf lettuce
1 small cucumber, thinly sliced
2 cups torn spinach
2 avocados, seeded, peeled, and sliced lengthwise
1 8-ounce package frozen cooked shrimp, thawed
Snipped chives (optional)
2 hard-cooked eggs, sliced

● For dressing, in a small mixing bowl combine mayonnaise or salad dressing, blue cheese, milk, lemon juice, and hot pepper sauce. Stir till well blended. Cover and chill.

● For salads, place iceberg lettuce in strips down the centers of 4 dinner plates. Combine sorrel and cucumber. Place sorrel mixture on one side of the lettuce and spinach on the other side of the lettuce. Arrange avocado slices in a fan shape on top of lettuce. Mound shrimp on top of lettuce near avocado. Spoon dressing on top of shrimp. If desired, sprinkle with snipped chives. Garnish with egg slices. Makes 4 servings.

Seafood-Pear Salads

For a different look, arrange the pear slices in a fan shape.

4 medium pears, halved lengthwise and cored
Lemon juice
½ cup mayonnaise *or* salad dressing
⅓ cup plain yogurt
¼ cup finely chopped seeded cucumber
1 tablespoon finely chopped onion
Bibb lettuce *or* Boston lettuce leaves
12 ounces frozen crab-flavored fish sticks, thawed and cut into 1-inch pieces
¾ cup plain croutons
Watercress sprigs (optional)

● Chop 1 pear half. Brush cut surfaces of remaining pear halves with lemon juice to prevent browning.

● For dressing, in a small mixing bowl combine the chopped pear, mayonnaise or salad dressing, yogurt, cucumber, and onion. Cover and chill while preparing salads.

● For salads, line 4 salad plates with lettuce leaves. Slice remaining pears lengthwise. If desired, brush cut edges of pears with additional lemon juice to prevent browning. Arrange pear slices in spoke fashion on the plates. Mound fish pieces in the centers of the pears. Spoon dressing over fish and sprinkle with croutons. If desired, garnish with watercress sprigs. Serves 4.

Gingered Shrimp Salads

Bias slice carrots and celery by holding the knife at a 45-degree angle.

1½ pounds fresh *or* frozen
    large shrimp in shells
¾ cup salad oil
¼ cup white wine vinegar
2 tablespoons water
½ teaspoon finely shredded
    lemon peel
1 tablespoon lemon juice
1½ teaspoons ground ginger
1 teaspoon sugar
½ teaspoon salt
2 cups thinly bias-sliced
    celery
2 cups thinly bias-sliced
    carrots
2 cups radish sprouts *or* fresh
    bean sprouts (see tip,
    page 66) *or* shredded
    Chinese cabbage

● Thaw shrimp, if frozen. Peel and devein shrimp. In a large saucepan combine 3 cups *water* and ½ teaspoon *salt.* Bring to boiling. Add shrimp. Cover and simmer for 1 to 3 minutes or till shrimp turn pink, then drain. Cool shrimp until they are easy to handle. Cut shrimp lengthwise in half. Place in a plastic bag. Place bag in a bowl.

● For dressing, in a screw-top jar combine oil, vinegar, water, lemon peel, lemon juice, ginger, sugar, and salt. Cover and shake well. Pour *half* of the dressing over the shrimp. Close bag and marinate in the refrigerator for 6 hours or overnight, turning bag occasionally. In another plastic bag place celery and carrots. Set bag in another bowl. Pour the remaining dressing over vegetables. Close bag and marinate in the refrigerator for 6 hours or overnight, turning bag occasionally.

● For salads, drain vegetables and mound them in the centers of 4 salad plates. Then arrange sprouts or Chinese cabbage around outer edges of plates. Drain shrimp. Lay shrimp, cut side down, in a circle on top of each vegetable mound. Serves 4.

Arranging the Gingered Shrimp Salads

It's easy to make these salads look elegant. First mound the celery and carrots in the centers of the salad plates. Then take your pick of sprouts or shredded Chinese cabbage and place it around the outer edges of the plates. (We used radish sprouts in the photo.) Finally, lay the shrimp, cut side down, in a circle on top of each vegetable mound.

Super Salad Bowls

½ cup wheat berries
¼ cup chopped celery
⅓ cup mayonnaise *or* salad
    dressing
⅓ cup plain yogurt
2 tablespoons thinly sliced
    green onion
1 teaspoon snipped fresh dill
    or ¼ teaspoon dried
    dillweed
½ teaspoon dried basil,
    crushed
⅛ teaspoon pepper
3 heads Bibb lettuce
1 7-ounce can solid white
    tuna, drained
2 small carrots, shredded
8 radishes, shredded
1 tablespoon milk

● In a small saucepan combine wheat berries and 2 cups *water*. Bring to boiling, then reduce heat. Cover and simmer for 1 hour. Drain and cool. In a medium mixing bowl combine the wheat berries and celery.

● For dressing, in a small mixing bowl combine mayonnaise or salad dressing, yogurt, onion, dill, basil, and pepper. Stir till well blended. Add *half* of the dressing mixture to the wheat berry mixture and toss lightly to coat. Cover and chill the wheat berry mixture and the remaining dressing separately.

● For salads, remove centers from heads of lettuce, leaving the outer leaves intact to form bowls. (Reserve centers for another use.) Place the lettuce bowls on 3 dinner plates. Break tuna into chunks. Arrange the wheat berry mixture, tuna, carrots, and radishes in separate piles in the lettuce bowls. If desired, garnish salads with additional fresh dill. If necessary, stir milk into the remaining dressing to make it of drizzling consistency. Serve remaining dressing separately. Makes 3 servings.

Aioli Platter

2 large carrots
1 9-ounce package frozen
    artichoke hearts
2 4- to 6-ounce fresh halibut
    steaks (cut 1 inch thick)
½ cup dry white wine
1 egg
2 tablespoons lemon juice
3 *or* 4 cloves garlic, chopped
¼ teaspoon salt
½ cup salad oil
½ cup olive oil
    Romaine leaves
4 hard-cooked eggs, sliced
1 cup whole fresh mushrooms
1 cup cherry tomatoes, halved
½ cup pitted ripe olives
    Milk
    Snipped chives (optional)

● Cut carrots crosswise in half, then cut pieces lengthwise in half. In a medium covered saucepan cook carrots and artichoke hearts in a small amount of lightly salted boiling water about 10 minutes or till vegetables are nearly tender, then drain. Rinse with cold water, then drain again. Cover and chill.

● Place fish in a small skillet. Add wine. Bring to boiling; reduce heat. Cover and simmer about 6 minutes or till fish flakes easily with a fork. Drain fish, cool, break into chunks, then chill.

● For dressing, in a blender container or food processor bowl combine the 1 egg, lemon juice, garlic, and salt. Cover and blend or process for 5 seconds. Through opening in lid and with blender or processor on slow speed, *gradually* add salad oil in a thin stream. (When necessary, stop blender and scrape sides.) Then on slow speed, *gradually* add olive oil in a thin stream.

● For salad, line a medium platter with romaine leaves. Arrange carrots, artichokes, fish, egg slices, mushrooms, tomatoes, and olives on the platter. If necessary, stir a few tablespoons of milk into dressing to make it of drizzling consistency. Drizzle some of the dressing over salad. If desired, sprinkle with snipped chives. Serve the remaining dressing separately. Makes 4 servings.

Super Salad Bowls

Sizzling Cheese Salad

You choose which cheese to "sizzle" in the skillet. Gjetost (YED-ohst) has a sweet caramellike flavor; feta (FEHT-uh) has a sharp salty flavor.

1 egg
1 tablespoon water
2 tablespoons yellow cornmeal
1 tablespoon fine dry bread crumbs
1 tablespoon sesame seed, toasted
2 teaspoons grated Parmesan cheese
4 ounces Neufchâtel cheese *or* cream cheese, cut up
1 cup shredded gjetost *or* crumbled feta cheese
6 cups torn mixed greens
1 medium tomato, cut into 8 wedges
¼ cup pitted ripe olives
¼ cup salad oil
¼ cup tarragon vinegar
1 tablespoon thinly sliced green onion
1 teaspoon Dijon-style mustard
1 tablespoon butter *or* margarine
1 tablespoon cooking oil
4 small pita bread rounds, split horizontally and toasted

● In a small shallow bowl combine egg and water. In another small shallow bowl combine cornmeal, bread crumbs, sesame seed, and Parmesan cheese. Set the mixtures aside.

● In a small mixer bowl combine the Neufchâtel or cream cheese and gjetost or feta cheese. Beat with an electric mixer on medium speed till well combined. Shape mixture into 1-inch balls. Dip cheese balls into egg mixture, then coat with the cornmeal mixture. Flatten balls to form patties. Cover and chill for 1 to 2 hours or till patties are firm.

● Meanwhile, on a large serving platter arrange the mixed greens, tomato wedges, and olives. Cover and chill while preparing dressing and frying cheese patties.

● For dressing, in a screw-top jar combine salad oil, vinegar, onion, and mustard. Cover and shake well. Set dressing aside.

● To fry cheese patties, in a skillet heat butter or margarine and cooking oil. Add cheese patties. Cook over medium heat, carefully turning once, for 2 to 3 minutes or till golden.

● To serve, shake dressing and drizzle it over greens on platter. Arrange the cheese patties on top. Serve with toasted pita rounds. Makes 4 servings.

SALADS

MARINATED OR MOLDED

Some of these salads are marinated and some are molded. But *all* of them are marvelous! By calling for just the right blend of herbs, wines, vinegars, and fruit juices, each recipe unlocks the secret to a wonderful flavor.

Salad-Making Hints

Kitchen Cut-Ups

Do terms like cubing and chopping or grating and shredding leave you wondering? The following guide explains some often-used (and confused) terms.

● To *cube* food, use a sharp knife and cut the food into lengthwise strips. Then cut each strip crosswise, forming uniformly sized pieces of food.

● To *chop* food, use a knife, blender, or food processor and cut the food into irregularly sized pieces.

● To cut food into *julienne* sticks, first cut the food into slices about 2 inches long and ¼ to ½ inch thick.

Stack the slices, then slice lengthwise again to form matchstick-size pieces.

● To *bias slice* vegetables, hold a sharp knife at a 45-degree angle while slicing.

● To *snip* fresh herbs or other foods, simply cut them with kitchen shears instead of a knife.

● To *shred* cheeses or citrus peels, rub them across a shredding surface. To shred cabbage or iceberg lettuce, simply slice it very thin.

● To *grate* hard cheese, rub it against a grating surface. Grating makes very fine particles which are easier to distribute in a salad.

Super-Easy Marinating

Here's the easiest ever way to marinate—it's one-step and requires no cleanup.

Place the food to be marinated in a clear plastic bag. Then set the bag in a deep bowl to support it.

Pour the dressing or marinade over the food in the bag. Close the bag, turning it to distribute the dressing or marinade evenly. Marinate the food in the refrigerator for as long as directed, turning the bag occasionally.

Use a slotted spoon to drain the marinated meat or vegetables, if necessary. Then either use the marinade as directed or close the bag and discard it.

Steak Salads

French bread with dilled butter completes this hearty meal. (Pictured on the cover.)

1 pound boneless beef sirloin
   steak, cut 1 inch thick
1 14-ounce can hearts of
   palm, drained and cut
   into bite-size pieces
1 cup cherry tomatoes, halved
½ cup thinly bias-sliced carrot
¼ cup bias-sliced green onion
⅓ cup salad oil
¼ cup white wine vinegar
2 teaspoons Dijon-style
   mustard
½ teaspoon finely shredded
   lemon peel
½ teaspoon dried dillweed
3 cups torn romaine
2 cups torn iceberg lettuce
2 cups torn curly endive
¾ cup sliced fresh mushrooms

● Slash fat edges of steak at 1-inch intervals, being careful not to cut into the meat. Place steak on the rack of an unheated broiler pan. Broil 3 inches from heat for 12 to 15 minutes for medium doneness, turning once. Cool and cut into thin slices. Place steak slices in a plastic bag. Place bag in a bowl; set aside.

● In another plastic bag place hearts of palm, tomatoes, carrot, and green onion. Place bag in another bowl and set aside.

● For dressing, in a screw-top jar combine oil, vinegar, mustard, lemon peel, dillweed, ½ teaspoon *salt,* and ¼ teaspoon *pepper.* Cover and shake well. Pour *half* of the dressing over meat. Pour remaining dressing over vegetables. Close bags. Marinate in the refrigerator for 6 hours or overnight, turning bags occasionally.

● For salads, in a large mixing bowl combine lettuces, endive, and mushrooms. Place the lettuce mixture on 4 plates. Arrange steak and vegetable mixtures on top of lettuce mixture. If desired, garnish with chives and lemon peel strips. Serves 4.

Chicken, Noodle, and Cabbage Slaw

It's crunchy! The cabbage stays crisp in this marinated salad.

1 3-ounce package Oriental
   noodles with chicken
   flavor
2 cups chopped cooked
   chicken
2 cups finely shredded
   cabbage
¼ cup sliced green onion
3 tablespoons sesame seed,
   toasted
¼ cup salad oil
3 tablespoons rice vinegar
   or white wine vinegar
1 tablespoon sugar
¼ teaspoon salt
¼ teaspoon pepper
1½ cups halved cherry
   tomatoes
2 tablespoons sliced almonds,
   toasted
   Green pepper rings

● Set aside the chicken seasoning package from the noodles. Break dry noodles into pieces. Cook noodles according to package directions, then drain. Rinse with cold water. Drain well.

● Place cooked noodles, chicken, cabbage, onion, and sesame seed in a plastic bag. Place bag in a bowl.

● For dressing, in a screw-top jar combine the chicken seasoning package, oil, vinegar, sugar, salt, and pepper. Cover and shake well to dissolve seasonings. Pour dressing over noodle mixture. Close bag and marinate in the refrigerator for 6 hours or overnight, turning bag occasionally.

● To serve, transfer mixture to a large salad bowl. Add tomatoes and toss lightly to mix. Sprinkle with almonds and garnish with green pepper rings. Makes 4 servings.

Marinated Antipasto Salads

A traditional Italian appetizer turned into an entrée.

2 cups cauliflower flowerets
1 medium zucchini, cut into
    ½-inch-thick slices
2 cups cherry tomatoes,
    halved
½ of a 6-ounce can pitted
    ripe olives, drained
1 ¾-ounce envelope garlic
    and herbs *or* Italian dry
    salad dressing mix
    Small romaine leaves
4 ounces thinly sliced
    prosciutto
5 ounces sliced cooked
    turkey, cut into bite-size
    strips (1 cup)
6 round slices Colby cheese,
    halved (about 5 ounces)
3 round slices provolone
    cheese, quartered (about
    4 ounces)

● In a large covered saucepan cook cauliflower in a small amount of boiling water for 2 minutes. Add zucchini and continue cooking about 2 minutes more or till vegetables are nearly tender. Drain and cool slightly. Place the cauliflower, zucchini, tomatoes, and olives in a plastic bag. Place bag in a bowl.

● Prepare salad dressing mix according to package directions. Pour dressing over vegetables. Close bag and marinate in the refrigerator for 6 hours or overnight, turning bag occasionally.

● For salads, line 6 salad plates with romaine leaves. Roll up each slice of prosciutto jelly-roll style. Drain vegetables, reserving dressing. Arrange the prosciutto, vegetables, turkey, and Colby and provolone cheeses on top of romaine. Serve reserved dressing separately. Makes 6 servings.

Seviche Salad

Forget the cooking. The lemon juice "cooks" the fish for you.

1 pound fresh *or* frozen
    haddock fillets, *or* peeled
    and deveined shrimp
¾ cup lemon juice *or* lime juice
1 9-ounce package frozen
    French-style green beans
5 cups torn iceberg lettuce
1 cup bias-sliced celery
1 2-ounce jar sliced pimiento,
    drained
2 tablespoons sliced green
    onion
¼ cup salad oil
2 tablespoons sugar
1 tablespoon snipped cilantro
    or parsley

● Thaw fish or shrimp, if frozen. Cut fish into ¾-inch cubes. Place *uncooked* fish or shrimp in a plastic bag. Place bag in a bowl. Pour lemon juice or lime juice over fish. Close bag. Marinate in the refrigerator for 24 hours, turning bag occasionally.

● Meanwhile, cook frozen beans according to package directions. Drain beans, then cover and chill.

● Drain fish or shrimp, reserving ½ *cup* of the lemon juice or lime juice. In a large salad bowl combine fish or shrimp, chilled beans, lettuce, celery, pimiento, and onion. Cover and chill while preparing dressing.

● For dressing, in a screw-top jar combine the reserved lemon juice or lime juice, oil, sugar, and cilantro or parsley. Cover and shake well. Pour dressing over lettuce mixture. Toss lightly to coat. Makes 6 servings.

Teriyaki Tofu Salad

1 16-ounce package tofu
   (fresh bean curd)
1 15-ounce can garbanzo
   beans, drained
2 cups sliced fresh
   mushrooms
1 small green pepper, cut into
   bite-size pieces
1 small tomato, seeded and
   chopped
⅓ cup sliced green onion
¼ cup snipped parsley
¼ cup olive oil *or* salad oil
¼ cup red wine vinegar
2 tablespoons Dijon-style
   mustard
1 teaspoon soy sauce
½ teaspoon ground ginger
1 clove garlic, minced
   Leaf lettuce

● Place the tofu in a double thickness of cheesecloth or paper towels. Press gently to extract as much moisture from tofu as possible. Cut tofu into ¾-inch cubes.

● Place tofu cubes, garbanzo beans, mushrooms, green pepper, tomato, onion, and parsley in a plastic bag. Set bag in a bowl.

● For dressing, in a screw-top jar combine oil, vinegar, mustard, soy sauce, ginger, garlic, and ½ teaspoon *salt*. Cover and shake well. Pour over bean mixture. Close bag and marinate in the refrigerator for 6 hours or overnight, turning bag occasionally.

● To serve, line 4 salad plates with lettuce leaves. Drain bean mixture and spoon it onto the plates. If desired, sprinkle with toasted sesame seed. Makes 4 servings.

Lasagna-Wrapped Salmon Salad

9 lasagna noodles
1 15½-ounce can salmon,
   drained, skin and bones
   removed, and flaked
2 green onions, thinly sliced
1½ cups alfalfa sprouts
1 cup chopped seeded
   cucumber
1 medium tomato, seeded and
   chopped
1 8-ounce can water
   chestnuts, drained and
   chopped
1 8-ounce package cream
   cheese, softened
¾ cup creamy buttermilk
   salad dressing
1 teaspoon dried dillweed
2 small tomatoes, thinly
   sliced
   Watercress sprig
   (optional)

● Cook noodles according to package directions, then drain. Rinse with cold water, then drain again. Set noodles aside.

● In a bowl combine salmon and onions. In another bowl combine sprouts, cucumber, chopped tomato, and water chestnuts.

● Stir together cream cheese, salad dressing, and dillweed till well blended. Stir ½ *cup* of the dressing mixture into salmon mixture. Stir ½ *cup* dressing mixture into sprout mixture.

● To assemble salad, line an 8- or 9-inch springform pan with noodles, extending noodles over sides of pan. Layer *half* of the salmon mixture on top of noodles in the pan, then layer all of the sprout mixture. Top with the remaining salmon mixture. Trim noodles so that 1½ inches extend over sides of pan. Discard trimmings. Fold ends of noodles over top of salmon layer. Spread remaining dressing mixture on top of the noodles to within 1 inch of the edge. Cover and chill for 2 to 4 hours.

● To serve, remove sides from pan. Leave salad on bottom of pan. Place on serving plate. Arrange tomato slices on top. If desired, garnish with watercress. Makes 8 servings.

Lasagna noodles mold this refreshing dill-salmon salad.

1 Arranging the noodles
When you're ready to assemble the Lasagna-Wrapped Salmon Salad, place the end of the first noodle in the center of an 8- or 9-inch springform pan, then extend the noodle over the side of the pan. Place the remaining noodles in the pan, spoke fashion. One end of each noodle should extend over the edge of the pan. The other ends of the noodles should overlap just slightly in the center of the pan so the filling won't leak out.

2 Serving the salad
To serve the salad, remove the sides from the springform pan. For easy serving, leave the salad on the bottom of the pan and place the pan bottom on a serving plate. Arrange the tomato slices in a ring on top of the salad. If desired, garnish with watercress. Then cut into wedges.

Shrimp-Rice Ring

Quick-thaw the frozen shrimp and peas by placing them in a colander and running cold tap water over them.

1¼ cups mayonnaise *or* salad dressing
3 tablespoons chopped sweet pickle
3 tablespoons white wine vinegar
2 tablespoons milk
1½ teaspoons prepared mustard *or* Dijon-style mustard
1⅓ cups long grain rice
2 6-ounce packages frozen cooked small shrimp, thawed
½ of a 10-ounce package (about 1 cup) frozen peas, thawed
1 small tomato, peeled, seeded, and chopped
½ cup chopped fresh mushrooms
½ cup chopped celery
½ cup thinly sliced green onion
¼ cup salad oil
2 tablespoons white wine vinegar
½ teaspoon sugar
½ teaspoon salt
Leaf lettuce
1 medium tomato, cut into wedges

● For sauce, in a small mixing bowl combine mayonnaise or salad dressing, pickle, 3 tablespoons wine vinegar, milk, and mustard. Stir till well blended. Cover and chill.

● Cook rice according to package directions. In a medium mixing bowl combine hot rice, shrimp, peas, chopped tomato, mushrooms, celery, and onion. Set rice mixture aside.

● In another small mixing bowl combine salad oil, 2 tablespoons wine vinegar, sugar, and salt. Stir till well blended. Stir *½ cup* of the sauce into the oil-vinegar mixture, then pour it over the rice mixture. Toss lightly to mix. Press rice mixture firmly into a lightly oiled 6½-cup ring mold. Cover and chill for 6 hours or overnight.

● To serve, line a platter with lettuce leaves. Invert mold onto platter. Give the mold a sharp tap, then lift mold off. (If necessary, wrap a warm dish towel around mold to loosen salad from mold.) Garnish with tomato wedges. Serve remaining sauce separately. Makes 6 servings.

IN·A·SHELL

For the ultimate
dinner-in-a-dish, serve your
salad in fruit, vegetable,
pastry, or tortilla shells.
Not only are these "bowls"
fun and attractive, but most
of them are edible. What a
great way to round out
your salad meal!

Salad-Making Hints

Two Ways to Cook Chicken For Salads

When a recipe calls for cooked chicken, you can use leftover roasted chicken or frozen diced chicken. If you don't have either of these on hand, here's how to substitute chicken breasts.

As a guide, use a small 8-ounce chicken breast for 4 ounces of cooked meat, a medium 12-ounce chicken breast for 5 ounces, and a large 1-pound chicken breast for 6½ ounces.

● *Poaching:* In a skillet bring about 1 inch of water to boiling. Carefully add the whole chicken breasts, then reduce the heat. Cover and simmer for 20 to 25 minutes or till the chicken breasts are tender.

Remove the chicken from the liquid. Cool the chicken slightly, then remove the skin and bones. Cut up the meat as directed.

● *Microwave:* Start with 2 whole medium chicken breasts. Place the chicken in a 1½-quart nonmetal casserole. *Don't add any liquid.* Micro-cook, covered, on 100% power (HIGH) for 2½ minutes. Turn chicken over. Micro-cook 2½ to 3½ minutes more or till tender. Cool, then remove skin and bones. Cut up meat as directed. (Timing is for 600- to 700-watt countertop microwave ovens. Time is approximate because ovens vary by manufacturer.)

Sprout Gardening In a Jar

You can grow sprouts at home in a dark corner of your cupboard. All you need is a 1-quart jar, cheesecloth, and seeds or beans. (Use alfalfa seeds, radish seeds, mung beans, soybeans, or lentils.)

Wash and sort ½ cup of seeds or beans, discarding the damaged ones. Soak them overnight in 2 cups of water (they may swell). Drain and rinse.

Place the soaked seeds or beans in the 1-quart jar. Then cover the top of the jar with two layers of cheesecloth, and fasten with a rubber band or string. Place the jar on its side so the seeds or beans form a shallow layer. Store the jar in a warm, dark place (68° to 75° F). Rinse the seeds or beans once daily in lukewarm water. Your sprouts should be ready to harvest in three to five days.

You can eat the whole sprout. But if you prefer to remove the hulls, place the sprouts in a bowl. Cover them with water and stir vigorously, skimming away the husks. Drain the sprouts and pat them dry with paper towels.

Taco Salads

No need to go to a restaurant when you're craving a taco salad.

8 cups torn iceberg lettuce
1 medium tomato, seeded and chopped
1 cup shredded cheddar cheese
¼ cup sliced pitted ripe olives
2 avocados, seeded and peeled
⅓ cup mayonnaise *or* salad dressing
2 slices bacon, crisp-cooked, drained, and crumbled
2 tablespoons chopped canned green chili peppers
1 tablespoon lemon juice
1 clove garlic, minced
1 pound ground beef
½ cup chopped onion
1 15½-ounce can red kidney beans, drained
1 8-ounce bottle hot taco sauce
Tortilla Bowls

● In a large mixing bowl combine lettuce, tomato, ¾ *cup* of the cheese, and olives. Toss lightly to mix. Cover and chill.

● For dressing, in a small mixing bowl mash avocados. Stir in the mayonnaise or salad dressing, bacon, green chili peppers, lemon juice, and garlic. If necessary, stir in 1 to 2 tablespoons *milk* to make dressing of desired consistency. Cover and chill.

● In a 10-inch skillet cook beef and onion till meat is brown and onion is tender. Drain off fat. Stir in beans and taco sauce. Cover and simmer for 10 minutes, stirring occasionally. Cool slightly.

● For salads, place lettuce mixture into tortilla bowls. Spoon warm meat mixture on top, then spoon dressing on top of meat. Sprinkle with remaining cheese. Makes 4 servings.

Tortilla Bowls: Cut eight 10-inch circles from *heavy* foil. In a large skillet heat four 10-inch *flour tortillas,* 1 at a time, over low heat for 1 minute or just till pliable. Place each tortilla on 2 foil circles. Bring foil up, shaping foil and tortillas together into ruffled bowls. (The foil acts as a support.) Place bowls onto an ungreased baking sheet. Bake in a 350° oven about 10 minutes or till crisp. Transfer bowls to a wire rack to cool. Remove foil.

Easy-Serve Salad Rolls

2 10-ounce packages brown-and-serve French rolls (each roll about 7 inches long)
⅓ cup sour cream dip with toasted onion
¼ cup mayonnaise *or* salad dressing
8 ounces desired sliced cold cuts (salami, boiled ham, *or* turkey breast), cut into 1½-inch julienne strips (about 1½ cups)
6 cherry tomatoes, quartered
½ cup chopped seeded cucumber
½ cup chopped celery
¼ cup chopped green pepper

● Bake 3 of the rolls according to package directions and cool. (Reserve remaining roll for another use.) For bread shells, cut a lengthwise slice from the top third of each baked roll. Hollow out the bottom of each roll, leaving a ½-inch-thick shell. (Reserve the bread from inside the shells for another use.) Place shells and tops in a plastic bag and set aside.

● For salad mixture, in a medium mixing bowl combine sour cream dip, mayonnaise or salad dressing, ¼ teaspoon *salt,* and ⅛ teaspoon *pepper.* Stir till well blended. Add cold cuts, tomatoes, cucumber, celery, and green pepper. Toss lightly to coat.

● Spoon salad mixture into bread shells, then cover with tops of rolls. Cut rolls crosswise in half. If desired, individually wrap rolls in foil and chill for no longer than 2 hours. Serves 6.

Corned Beef 'n' Cabbage Salads

Corned Beef 'n' Cabbage Salads

Treat friends to a mini-Oktoberfest. Serve this German-style salad in rye bread bowls.

1¼ to 1¾ cups all-purpose flour
1 package active dry yeast
½ cup milk
1 tablespoon molasses *or* honey
½ teaspoon salt
1 egg
1 cup shredded Monterey Jack cheese
¾ cup rye flour
1 beaten egg
3 cups shredded cabbage
6 ounces fully cooked corned beef brisket, cut into bite-size pieces (about 1⅓ cups)
4 ounces Swiss cheese, cut into 1-inch julienne sticks
1 medium apple, cored and chopped
½ cup shredded carrot
⅓ cup Thousand Island salad dressing
¼ cup mayonnaise *or* salad dressing
2 teaspoons Dijon-style mustard
1 teaspoon caraway seed

● For bread dough, in a small mixer bowl combine *1 cup* of the all-purpose flour and yeast. In a saucepan heat together milk, molasses or honey, and salt just till warm (115° to 120°). Add warm liquid to flour mixture, then add 1 egg and Monterey Jack cheese. Beat with an electric mixer on low speed for 30 seconds, scraping sides of bowl constantly. Beat 3 minutes at high speed. Using a spoon, stir in the rye flour and as much of remaining all-purpose flour as you can. Turn dough out onto a lightly floured surface. Knead in enough of the remaining all-purpose flour to make a moderately stiff dough that is smooth and elastic (6 to 8 minutes total). Place in a lightly greased bowl. Turn once to grease surface. Cover and let rise in a warm place till double (about 1 hour). Punch down. Cover *one-third* of the dough and set aside. Divide the remaining dough into 4 portions. Shape each portion of the dough into a smooth ball. Cover and let rest 10 minutes.

● For bread bowls, roll each of the 4 small balls of dough into an 8-inch circle. On lightly greased baking sheets, fit each dough circle over the bottom of an inverted, well-greased 10-ounce custard cup or individual casserole. Trim dough at edges of dishes. Smooth edges of dough, pressing against dishes. On a lightly floured surface roll the reserved dough into a 12x9-inch rectangle. Cut dough into leaves or other cutout shapes.

● Bake bread bowls in a 375° oven for 5 minutes. Brush with mixture of 1 beaten egg and 1 tablespoon *water*. Press cutouts onto edges of bowls. Brush cutouts with egg-water mixture. Return bowls to oven and bake for 5 to 7 minutes more or till golden. (If dough puffs up, press it down with a pot holder.) With a narrow metal spatula, remove bread from custard cups. Turn bowls right side up on the baking sheets. Brush insides of bowls and rims with egg-water mixture. Return to oven and bake for 5 minutes more. If necessary, cover the edges with foil to prevent overbrowning. Transfer bowls to a wire rack to cool. Store cooled bread bowls in a clear plastic bag till serving time.

● Meanwhile, for the salad mixture, in a medium mixing bowl combine cabbage, corned beef, Swiss cheese, apple, and carrot. In another mixing bowl combine Thousand Island dressing, mayonnaise or salad dressing, mustard, and caraway seed. Stir till well blended. Pour dressing over cabbage mixture. Toss lightly to coat. Cover and chill for 2 to 6 hours.

● To serve, place bread bowls on 4 salad plates. Fill with salad mixture. Makes 4 servings.

Deep-Dish Salad Pizza

Having a pizza party? Put away the tomato sauce and pull out the salad dressing. This version features chicken, spinach, and mushrooms in a puff pastry crust.

1   8-ounce container soft-style cream cheese with toasted onion

⅓   cup creamy Italian salad dressing

4   cups torn spinach

3   cups sliced fresh mushrooms

2   cups chopped cooked chicken

1   cup shredded carrot

1   2¼-ounce can sliced pitted ripe olives, drained

1   17¼-ounce package (2 sheets) frozen puff pastry, thawed

2   cups shredded provolone cheese *or* mozzarella cheese

2   cups shredded Gruyère cheese

1   avocado, seeded, peeled, and thinly sliced

1   medium tomato, thinly sliced

● For dressing, in a small mixer bowl combine cream cheese and Italian salad dressing. Beat with an electric mixer till smooth. (Dressing will be thick.) Set dressing aside.

● For the spinach mixture, in a large mixing bowl combine spinach, mushrooms, chicken, carrot, and olives. Toss lightly to mix. Cover and chill while preparing crust.

● For a 14-inch round pizza, on a lightly floured surface place 1 sheet of pastry on top of the other sheet, staggering the corners. Roll pastry from center to edge, forming a 16-inch circle. (For a 15½x10½-inch rectangular pizza, place pastry sheets on top of each other without staggering the corners. Roll out pastry, forming a 17x12-inch rectangle.) Wrap pastry around the rolling pin. Unroll pastry into a 14-inch deep-dish pizza pan (or a 15½x10½x2-inch baking pan), extending pastry about 1 inch up sides of pan. Prick bottom *well* with the tines of a fork. Bake in a 375° oven for 25 to 30 minutes or till golden brown.

● Combine provolone or mozzarella cheese and Gruyere cheese. Sprinkle *2½ cups* of the cheese mixture over the warm crust. Return crust to the oven and bake for 4 to 5 minutes more or till cheese begins to melt.

● Meanwhile, pour dressing over spinach mixture and toss lightly to coat. Spread spinach mixture over melted cheese on crust. Then sprinkle with remaining cheese mixture. Return to oven. Bake for 4 to 5 minutes more or till cheese is melted.

● Immediately garnish with avocado and tomato slices. Cut into wedges or squares to serve. Makes 10 to 12 servings.

Chicken 'n' Walnut Puff

One BIG cream puff shell filled with a tarragon chicken salad.

1 cup water
½ cup butter *or* margarine
1 cup all-purpose flour
4 eggs
3 cups shredded Chinese cabbage
2 cups finely chopped cooked chicken
¾ cup broken walnuts
⅓ cup shredded carrot
¼ cup thinly sliced green onion
⅔ cup mayonnaise *or* salad dressing
½ cup dairy sour cream
2 tablespoons vinegar
½ teaspoon dried tarragon, crushed
2 small cloves garlic, minced
½ of a 6-ounce package (about 1 cup) frozen pea pods, thawed (optional)

● For puff shell, in a medium saucepan bring water to boiling. Reduce heat. Add the butter or margarine and stir till melted. Add flour and ¼ teaspoon *salt* all at once, stirring vigorously. Cook and stir till the mixture forms a ball that doesn't separate. Remove from heat and cool slightly, about 5 minutes.

● Add eggs, 1 at a time, beating after each addition till smooth. Spread batter over the bottom and up the sides of a greased 10-inch pie plate or quiche dish. Bake in a 400° oven for 25 to 30 minutes or till golden brown and puffy. Leave the puff shell in the pie plate and cool it on a wire rack.

● Meanwhile, for salad mixture, in a large mixing bowl combine Chinese cabbage, chicken, walnuts, carrot, and onion.

● For dressing, in a small mixing bowl combine mayonnaise or salad dressing, sour cream, vinegar, tarragon, garlic, and ⅛ teaspoon *salt*. Stir till well blended. Pour over salad mixture. Toss lightly to coat. If desired, cover and chill for 30 minutes.

● To serve, spoon salad mixture into the puff shell. If desired, garnish with pea pods. Cut into wedges. Makes 6 servings.

Papaya Boats with Chicken

You choose: Either remove the peels from the papayas or leave them on.

2 papayas
3 cups chopped cooked chicken
2 tablespoons thinly sliced green onion
1 8-ounce carton dairy sour cream
2 tablespoons frozen orange juice concentrate, thawed
1 tablespoon snipped cilantro *or* 1 teaspoon ground coriander
½ teaspoon dry mustard
2 drops bottled hot pepper sauce
2 cups shredded iceberg lettuce (optional)
¼ cup coconut, toasted

● For papaya shells, use a sharp knife to cut the papayas lengthwise in half. Remove seeds. Cut out papaya pulp, leaving ¼-inch-thick shells. Cover and chill shells.

● Cut papaya pulp into ½-inch cubes. In a medium mixing bowl combine cubed papaya, chicken, and green onion.

● For the dressing, in a small mixing bowl combine sour cream, orange juice concentrate, cilantro or coriander, dry mustard, and hot pepper sauce. Stir till well blended. Pour dressing over chicken mixture. Toss lightly to coat. If desired, cover and chill the chicken mixture for up to 4 hours.

● To serve, if desired, arrange lettuce on 4 salad plates. Place the papaya shells onto the lettuce. Spoon chicken mixture into papaya shells. Sprinkle with toasted coconut. If desired, garnish with cilantro or parsley sprigs. Makes 4 servings.

**Poultry-Filled
Summertime Melons**

Chicken and Fruit Toss

A fruit lover's delight—pineapple shells filled with pineapple, oranges, kiwi fruit, and lettuce, all tossed in a tangerine dressing.

¼ cup water
¼ cup frozen tangerine juice
    concentrate
1 tablespoon lemon juice *or*
    lime juice
1 teaspoon cornstarch
2 small pineapples, chilled
2 cups shredded iceberg
    lettuce
1½ cups cubed cooked chicken
1 orange, peeled and
    sectioned
1 kiwi fruit, peeled, sliced, and
    quartered
2 ounces Monterey Jack
    cheese, cut into 1-inch
    julienne sticks

● For dressing, in a small saucepan combine water, tangerine juice concentrate, lemon or lime juice, and cornstarch. Cook and stir till thickened and bubbly. Cook and stir for 2 minutes more. Remove from heat. Cover surface with waxed paper or clear plastic wrap. Cool slightly *without* stirring, then chill.

● Meanwhile, for pineapple shells use a sharp knife to cut the pineapples lengthwise in half, crown and all. Remove hard cores from pineapples. Cut out pineapple meat, leaving shells intact. Set pineapple shells aside.

● Cut pineapple meat into bite-size chunks. Set aside *3 cups* of the chunks. (Refrigerate remaining pineapple for another use.)

● In a medium mixing bowl combine reserved pineapple chunks, lettuce, chicken, orange sections, kiwi fruit, and cheese. Pour dressing over fruit mixture. Toss lightly to coat.

● Immediately spoon fruit mixture into pineapple shells. Place shells on 4 salad plates. Makes 4 servings.

Poultry-Filled Summertime Melons

Prefer honeydew melons? Use them in place of the cantaloupes.

½ cup pineapple yogurt
2 tablespoons mayonnaise *or*
    salad dressing
¼ teaspoon ground ginger
2 cups cubed cooked
    chicken *or* turkey
½ cup sliced celery
2 small cantaloupes
    Leaf lettuce
1 cup strawberries, halved
1 tablespoon sunflower nuts
    Whole strawberries
    (optional)

● For salad mixture, in a medium mixing bowl combine yogurt, mayonnaise or salad dressing, and ginger. Stir till well blended. Add chicken or turkey and celery. Toss lightly to coat. If desired, cover and chill for up to 8 hours.

● Meanwhile, cut cantaloupes lengthwise in half. Remove seeds. Using a melon-ball cutter, scoop the pulp out of the cantaloupes. Set aside and chill *2 cups* of the cantaloupe balls till serving time. (Refrigerate remaining balls for another use.)

● If desired, lay the shells on their sides. Using the melon-ball cutter, press down onto edges of shells, cutting scalloped edges.

● To serve, line 4 salad plates with lettuce leaves. Place the cantaloupe shells on the plates. Divide the reserved cantaloupe balls among the shells. Mound salad mixture in centers. Place strawberry halves around the salad mixtures. Sprinkle with sunflower nuts. If desired, garnish the plates with whole strawberries. Makes 4 servings.

Curried Salad-Stuffed Artichokes

1 cup cooked rice
2 4½-ounce cans shrimp, rinsed and chopped
½ cup chopped celery
¼ cup raisins
2 green onions, thinly sliced
1 recipe Curry Dressing (see recipe, page 82)
1 to 2 tablespoons milk
6 large artichokes
Lemon juice
⅓ cup chopped peanuts

● For rice filling, in a medium mixing bowl combine rice, shrimp, celery, raisins, and onions. Add ⅔ *cup* of the Curry Dressing. Toss lightly to coat. Cover and chill about 3 hours.

● For dipping sauce, stir enough milk into remaining Curry Dressing to make it of dipping consistency. Cover and chill.

● Meanwhile, wash and remove the coarse outer leaves from artichokes. Trim stems even with bases, then slice off about 1 inch from tops. With shears, snip off about ½ inch from tips of remaining leaves. Brush lemon juice onto cut edges.

● In a large saucepan bring about 2 inches of lightly salted water to boiling. Add artichokes. Cover and boil gently about 20 minutes or till stem ends pierce easily with a fork, then drain. Cool artichokes until easy to handle. Pull out center leaves. Scoop out fuzzy centers (chokes). Cover and chill about 1 hour.

● To serve, stir peanuts into rice mixture. Spoon mixture into artichokes. (If necessary, spread center leaves open to fill.) Serve dipping sauce separately for dipping leaves. Makes 6 servings.

Preparing artichokes
First, wash and remove the coarse outer leaves from the artichokes. Then, with a sharp knife, trim the bottom stems so the artichokes sit flat. Cut off about a 1-inch slice from the top of each artichoke.

With kitchen shears, snip off about ½ inch from the tips of the remaining leaves. Brush lemon juice onto the cut edges to prevent browning.

By-the-Seashore Salmon Shells

Take a bite and close your eyes—you just might hear the waves hitting the rocks.

12 large shell macaroni
3 hard-cooked eggs
½ cup creamy buttermilk
   salad dressing
¼ teaspoon dried dillweed
1 15½-ounce can salmon,
   drained, skin and bones
   removed, flaked, and
   chilled
½ cup thinly sliced celery
4 cups shredded iceberg
   lettuce
1 medium green pepper,
   seeded and cut into strips
1 medium tomato, seeded and
   chopped
   Creamy buttermilk salad
   dressing

● Cook pasta shells according to package directions, then drain. Rinse with cold water, then drain again and chill.

● Meanwhile, cut hard-cooked eggs in half and remove yolks. In a medium mixing bowl mash yolks with a fork. Stir in the ½ cup buttermilk dressing and dillweed. Chop the egg whites. Add chopped egg whites, salmon, and celery to yolk mixture. Mix just till combined. If desired, cover and chill for up to 8 hours.

● In a medium mixing bowl combine shredded lettuce, green pepper, and chopped tomato. Toss lightly to mix.

● To serve, divide lettuce mixture among 4 salad plates. Spoon salmon mixture into pasta shells. Place 3 shells on top of lettuce on each plate. Serve additional buttermilk dressing separately. Makes 4 servings.

Tuna-Stuffed Tomatoes

You'll need big, plump tomatoes to hold all of this wonderful mint-tuna filling.

4 large tomatoes
¼ cup mayonnaise *or* salad
   dressing
¼ cup dairy sour cream
2 tablespoons thinly sliced
   green onion
4 teaspoons snipped fresh
   mint *or* 1½ teaspoons
   dried mint, crushed
1 12½-ounce can tuna,
   drained, broken into
   chunks, and chilled
½ cup chopped seeded
   cucumber
   Red leaf lettuce *or* alfalfa
   sprouts

● For tomato shells, cut a thin slice off the top of each tomato. Use a spoon to scoop out the seeds and pulp from each tomato, leaving a ¼-inch-thick shell. Invert shells onto paper towels to drain, then chill till serving time. Discard seeds from the scooped-out pulp. Chop the pulp, then drain. Reserve ½ *cup* of the drained pulp.

● For salad mixture, in a mixing bowl combine mayonnaise or salad dressing, sour cream, onion, and mint. Stir mixture till well blended. Add tuna and toss lightly to mix. If desired, cover and chill for up to 8 hours.

● To serve, add the reserved chopped tomato and cucumber to the salad mixture. Toss lightly to mix. Line 4 salad plates with lettuce leaves or sprouts. Place tomato shells on the plates. Fill the shells with salad mixture, mounding mixture slightly. Makes 4 servings.

Egg Salad in Tomato Tulips

Great taste and fewer calories! Your egg salad will have both when you use yogurt and dry cottage cheese instead of mayonnaise.

  1 cup dry cottage cheese
  ½ cup plain yogurt
  ½ teaspoon dried dillweed
  ¼ teaspoon salt
  ⅛ teaspoon pepper
  4 hard-cooked eggs, chopped
  ½ cup chopped celery
     Romaine leaves *or* alfalfa
        sprouts
  4 large tomatoes

● For egg salad mixture, in a medium mixing bowl combine the cottage cheese, yogurt, dillweed, salt, and pepper. Stir in eggs and celery. If desired, cover and chill for up to 8 hours.

● To serve, line 4 salad plates with romaine leaves or arrange sprouts on plates. Cut out ½ inch of the core from each tomato. Invert tomatoes. Cutting from the top to, *but not through,* the stem end, cut each tomato into 6 wedges. Place tomatoes on the plates. Spread wedges slightly apart, then fill with egg salad mixture. Makes 4 servings.

Making tomato tulips
Choose large fresh tomatoes to make attractive cups for individual servings of salad. Make the cups by inserting the point of a sharp knife into each tomato near the core. Then cut out ½ inch of the core. Invert the tomatoes. Cutting from the top to, *but not through,* the stem end, cut each tomato into 6 wedges. Place tomatoes on the plates. Spread wedges slightly apart, then fill with the salad mixture.

DRESSING-IT-UP

They're the tops! Try our Herb Vinegar, Nut-Flavored Oil, Homemade Mayonnaise, or Thousand Island Dressing with the salad recipes in this book. Or create your own salad using one of these toppings. Then, for a touch of class, add our Parmesan Croutons or Marinated Cheese cubes.

Salad-Making Hints

Oil Options

Your choices in salad oils are many. Read below and we'll tell you their differences.

● *Vegetable oil* or *salad oil* is light yellow in color and bland in flavor. It's usually made from corn, soybeans, sunflowers, or peanuts.

● *Olive oil* is made from pressed olives. You can buy different grades of olive oil. "Extra virgin" oil meets the highest standards. It contains less than one percent of oleic acid, and has a full-bodied, rich aroma and flavor. "Virgin" oil has slightly lower standards. Its maximum content of oleic acid is 3.3 percent. "Pure" oil is made by blending substandard olive oils with "extra virgin" or "virgin" olive oil.

Even within these broad categories, differences in color and flavor exist. Green to greenish gold olive oil, pressed from green, semi-ripe olives, is slightly sharp tasting. Golden olive oil, pressed from ripe olives, is more delicately flavored.

● *Nut oils* are pressed from walnuts, hazelnuts, or almonds. Buy these nut oils in a specialty shop or make your own Nut-Flavored Oil (see recipe, opposite). Of the three, hazelnut oil has the most pronounced nut flavor, while almond oil has the mildest nut flavor.

● *Sesame oil* is found in Oriental stores or large supermarkets. It is pressed from toasted sesame seed. Because this oil has so much flavor, use only a few drops in your dressing.

A Vinegar for Every Taste

Red or white, fruity or tangy, pungent or sweet—vinegars come in many varieties, strengths, colors, and flavors.

● *Cider vinegar* is golden brown in color. It has a strong bite with a faint apple flavor.

● *Distilled* or *white vinegar* is colorless and has a very sharp taste. Use this vinegar when you don't want to change the color of your food, such as in salads containing rice, pasta, poultry, or fish.

● *Wine vinegar* is made from champagne, sherry, or white, red, or rosé wine. Like the wine it's made from, red wine vinegar has a more full-bodied flavor than white wine vinegar. Choose the type of wine vinegar that best complements the colors and flavors of your salad.

● *Balsamic vinegar* is made by pressing highly sugared grapes and cooking the resulting liquid in copper caldrons. The cooked liquid is then aged in wooden barrels for at least 10 years. This process results in a delicate sweet flavor.

● *Flavored vinegar* has the added flavor of fruits or herbs. It is made from cider, distilled, or wine vinegar. You can buy these vinegars or make them yourself (see recipes, pages 79 and 80). Use them just as you would other vinegars. Just be sure to use the flavored vinegar that best complements the flavors in your salad.

Nut-Flavored Oil

A nutty aroma with the flavor of almond, hazelnut, or walnut. (Pictured on page 81.)

1½ cups unblanched whole
    almonds, hazelnuts, *or*
    walnuts (about 7½
    ounces)
2½ cups salad oil

● In a blender container or food processor bowl place nuts. Cover and blend or process till chopped. Through the opening in the lid, and with blender or processor on slow speed, gradually add *½ cup* of oil. Blend or process till nuts are finely chopped.

● Transfer nut mixture to a small saucepan. Clip a candy or deep-fat cooking thermometer onto the side of the pan. Cook over low heat, stirring occasionally, till thermometer registers 160°. Remove from heat and cool slightly. Combine the nut mixture with the remaining salad oil in a jar or bottle. Cover tightly and let stand in a cool place for 1 to 2 weeks before using.

● To use, line a colander with fine-woven cloth or a cup-shaped coffee filter. Pour oil mixture through the colander and let mixture drain into a bowl. Discard nut paste. Transfer the strained liquid to a 1½-pint jar or bottle. If desired, add a few whole nuts to the jar or label for identification.

● To store the Nut-Flavored Oil, refrigerate, tightly covered, for up to 3 months. Makes about 2½ cups.

Herb Vinegar

Just sprinkle on top of greens. This flavorful vinegar can stand alone.

2 cups tightly packed fresh
    herb leaves *or* sprigs
    (tarragon, thyme,
    dill, mint, *or* basil)
2 cups vinegar
    Fresh herb sprig (optional)

● Pack 2 cups herbs into a hot, clean 1-quart jar.

● In a stainless steel or enamel saucepan heat vinegar till hot, *but not boiling.* Pour the hot vinegar over herbs in jar. Cover loosely with a glass, plastic, or cork lid till mixture cools. (The vinegar would erode metal lids.) Then cover tightly with the lid. Let vinegar stand in a cool, dark place for 1 week before using.

● To store the Herb Vinegar, remove herbs from jar. If desired, transfer liquid to a clean 1-pint jar or bottle. Either label or add an additional sprig of fresh herb to the jar for identification. Cover tightly with a glass, plastic, or cork lid. Place in a cool, dark place for up to 3 months. Makes 2 cups.

Orange Vinegar: Prepare the Herb Vinegar as directed above, *except* use *white wine vinegar* and omit the fresh herbs. Heat vinegar with three 3x½-inch strips *orange peel* (white membrane removed). Transfer hot vinegar and peel to a hot, clean 1-pint jar or bottle. Cover and let vinegar stand in a cool, dark place for 4 to 5 days before using. To store vinegar, remove peel.

Raspberry-Mint Vinegar

2 teaspoons dried mint, crushed, *or* four 3- to 4-inch fresh mint sprigs

½ of a 12-ounce package lightly sweetened frozen red raspberries *or* 1½ cups fresh raspberries

2 cups cider vinegar

1 cup dry red wine

● Place mint in a clean 1-quart jar. Set jar aside. Thaw raspberries, if frozen. (Or thoroughly rinse fresh raspberries with cold water, then drain well.) In a stainless steel or enamel saucepan bring the raspberries, vinegar, and wine to boiling. Boil gently, uncovered, for 3 minutes.

● Pour hot mixture over mint in jar. Cover; let stand in a cool, dark place for 1 week. Line a colander with fine-woven cloth or a cup-shaped coffee filter. Pour mixture through the colander and let drain into a bowl. Transfer the strained liquid to a clean 1½-pint jar or bottle. Cover tightly with a glass, plastic, or cork lid. Store in the refrigerator for up to 6 months. Makes 3 cups.

Basic Vinaigrette

½ cup olive oil *or* salad oil

¼ cup wine vinegar

1 teaspoon sugar

½ teaspoon salt

½ teaspoon dry mustard

1 small clove garlic, minced

● In a screw-top jar combine oil, wine vinegar, sugar, salt, dry mustard, and garlic. Cover and shake well.

● To store, refrigerate, tightly covered, for up to 1 month. (If you make the vinaigrette with olive oil, bring back to room temperature before serving.) Shake again before serving. Makes ¾ cup.

Tomato Vinaigrette: Prepare Basic Vinaigrette as directed above, *except* add ¼ cup canned *tomato puree* and 1½ teaspoons snipped *fresh basil* or *thyme, or* ½ teaspoon *dried basil* or *thyme,* crushed. To store, refrigerate, tightly covered, for up to 2 weeks. Makes about 1 cup.

Low-Cal Italian Dressing

This oil-less dressing has only 3 calories per 2-tablespoon serving.

2 tablespoons liquid fruit pectin

2 tablespoons finely chopped onion

¼ teaspoon garlic salt

¼ teaspoon dried basil, crushed

⅛ teaspoon dried oregano, crushed

⅛ teaspoon crushed red pepper

2 tablespoons cider vinegar

● In a small mixing bowl combine fruit pectin, onion, garlic salt, basil, oregano, and crushed red pepper. Stir in vinegar and ½ cup *water.* Cover and refrigerate overnight before using.

● To store, transfer dressing to a ½-pint bottle or jar. Refrigerate, tightly covered, for up to 3 days. Shake before serving. Makes about ⅔ cup.

Nut-Flavored Oil
(see recipe, page 79)

Raspberry-Mint Vinegar

Tomato Vinaigrette

Low-Cal Italian Dressing

Thousand Island Dressing
(see recipe, page 85)

Dill 'n' Chive Dressing
(see recipe, page 86)

Homemade Mayonnaise

2 egg yolks
2 tablespoons vinegar
½ teaspoon salt
½ teaspoon dry mustard
¼ teaspoon paprika
Dash ground red pepper
2 cups salad oil
2 tablespoons lemon juice

● In a small mixer bowl combine egg yolks, vinegar, salt, mustard, paprika, and red pepper. Beat with an electric mixer on low speed till blended. Add oil *1 teaspoon* at a time, beating on medium speed till *¼ cup* has been added. Then *gradually* add remaining oil in a thin stream, alternating the last *½ cup* of oil with lemon juice. Use as a spread, in salad dressings, or in the recipes below. To store, refrigerate, covered, up to 1 month (2 weeks for the Horseradish-Mustard Dressing). Makes 2½ cups.

Horseradish-Mustard Dressing: Stir together 1 cup *Homemade Mayonnaise,* 1 tablespoon prepared *horseradish,* and 1 teaspoon *dry mustard.* Fold in ½ cup *whipping cream,* whipped. Serve on beef or pork salads. Makes 1¾ cups.

Coral Dressing: Stir together 1 cup *Homemade Mayonnaise,* ⅓ cup *chili sauce,* ½ teaspoon finely shredded *lemon peel,* and 1 teaspoon *lemon juice.* Serve on seafood salads. Makes 1⅓ cups.

Curry Dressing: Stir together 1 cup *Homemade Mayonnaise,* ¼ cup *chutney,* 1 tablespoon *milk,* and 2 teaspoons *curry powder.* Serve on meat, poultry, or seafood salads. Makes 1¼ cups.

1 Adding salad oil by the teaspoon

With the electric mixer on medium speed, add salad oil *1 teapoon* at a time to the yolk mixture. Continue beating until *¼ cup* (12 teaspoons) of the salad oil has been added.

This step assures that the oil will not separate out of the finished mayonnaise.

2 Adding remaining salad oil

While continuing to beat the mixture with the electric mixer, *gradually* pour in the remaining salad oil in a thin, steady stream (slightly less than ⅛ inch in diameter) till all but *½ cup* has been added. Scrape the sides of the bowl occasionally.

Add the last ½ cup of oil alternately with the lemon juice, beating at medium speed till thoroughly blended. It should take you 12 to 15 minutes to add all of the salad oil and lemon juice.

3 Checking the consistency

Your finished Homemade Mayonnaise should be smooth, yet thick enough to hold a cut edge and to mound on itself, as shown.

If your mayonnaise separates or appears thin or curdled, restore it by *very slowly* beating the separated mixture into an egg yolk. This remedy will not work if you reverse the procedure and beat the yolk into the separated mayonnaise mixture.

Parmesan, Italian, Dill Croutons
(see recipes, page 87)

Lemon-Marinated Olives
(see recipe, page 86)

Marinated Cheese
(see recipe, page 87)

84

Low-Cal Blue Cheese Dressing

On a diet? You won't be cheating with this rich-tasting, creamy dressing. It's only 25 calories for a 2-tablespoon serving.

1 cup low-fat cottage cheese
½ cup buttermilk
¼ cup crumbled blue cheese
½ teaspoon Worcestershire sauce
⅛ teaspoon garlic powder
3 drops bottled hot pepper sauce
  Buttermilk

● In a blender container or food processor bowl place cottage cheese, ½ cup buttermilk, blue cheese, Worcestershire sauce, garlic powder, and bottled hot pepper sauce. Cover and blend or process about 45 seconds or till smooth. If necessary, stir in a few tablespoons of additional buttermilk to make dressing of desired consistency.

● To store, refrigerate, tightly covered, for up to 1 week. Stir before serving. Makes about 1½ cups.

Thousand Island Dressing

Save 89 calories per 2-tablespoon serving by using reduced-calorie mayonnaise. (Dressing pictured on page 81.)

1 cup mayonnaise *or* salad dressing
2 tablespoons chili sauce
1 hard-cooked egg, finely chopped
2 tablespoons chopped dill pickle
2 tablespoons diced pimiento
1 green onion, thinly sliced
1 teaspoon prepared horseradish
  Several drops bottled hot pepper sauce
2 to 4 tablespoons milk

● In a small mixing bowl combine the mayonnaise or salad dressing and chili sauce. Stir in egg, pickle, pimiento, green onion, horseradish, and hot pepper sauce. Stir in enough milk to make dressing of desired consistency. If desired, cover and chill the dressing before serving.

● To store, refrigerate, tightly covered, for up to 1 week. Stir before serving. Makes 1⅔ cups.

Buttermilk Dressing

Check your buttermilk carton for the expiration date. That's how long this dressing will keep.

1¼ cups mayonnaise *or* salad dressing
¾ cup buttermilk
1 tablespoon snipped chives
¼ teaspoon salt
¼ teaspoon onion powder
¼ teaspoon garlic powder
⅛ teaspoon white pepper

● In a mixing bowl combine mayonnaise or salad dressing and buttermilk. Stir till well blended. Stir in chives, salt, onion powder, garlic powder, and pepper. Cover and chill before serving.

● To store, refrigerate, tightly covered. Stir before serving. Makes 2 cups.

Creamy Cucumber Dressing

Leave out the milk and you've got a terrific vegetable dip.

½ cup mayonnaise *or* salad
    dressing
½ cup plain yogurt
1 tablespoon snipped chives
    or thinly sliced green
    onion
1 small cucumber, peeled,
    seeded, and finely
    chopped (about ¾ cup)
¼ to ½ cup milk

● In a small mixing bowl combine mayonnaise or salad dressing, yogurt, and chives or green onion. Stir till well blended. Add the chopped cucumber. Stir in enough milk to make dressing of desired consistency.

● To store, refrigerate, tightly covered, for up to 2 weeks. Stir before serving. Makes 1¾ cups.

Dill 'n' Chive Dressing

It's tangy, but so good! (Pictured on page 81.)

½ cup dairy sour cream
2 tablespoons white wine
    vinegar
1 teaspoon sugar
1 teaspoon dried dillweed
½ teaspoon salt
½ teaspoon dry mustard
1 small clove garlic, minced
⅓ cup salad oil
2 tablespoons snipped chives

● In a blender container or food processor bowl combine sour cream, vinegar, sugar, dillweed, salt, dry mustard, and garlic. Cover and blend or process for 5 seconds. Through the opening in the lid or with lid ajar, and with blender or processor on slow speed, *gradually* add oil in a thin stream. (When necessary, stop blender or processor and scrape sides.) Stir in chives.

● To store, refrigerate, tightly covered, for up to 1 week. Stir before serving. Makes 1 cup.

Lemon-Marinated Olives

Not only fantastic in a salad, but also wonderful as an anytime snack. (Pictured on page 84.)

1 5¾-ounce can pitted ripe
    jumbo olives, drained
¼ cup blanched whole
    almonds
1½ teaspoons coriander seed,
    crushed
⅓ cup water
⅓ cup dry white wine
2 tablespoons olive oil *or*
    salad oil
2 tablespoons lemon juice
    Lemon slices *and* lime slices
    (optional)

● Stuff the pitted olives with the whole almonds. Place stuffed olives in a screw-top 1-pint jar. Add coriander seed to jar.

● For marinade, in another screw-top jar combine water, wine, oil, and lemon juice. Cover and shake well. Pour marinade over olives. Cover and marinate in the refrigerator for 1 week before using, shaking the jar containing the olives occasionally.

● To serve, if desired, line a small serving bowl with lemon and lime slices. Using a slotted spoon, transfer olives to the bowl. Pass as a salad accompaniment. To store olives in the marinade, refrigerate, tightly covered, for up to 2 weeks. Makes 2 cups.

Marinated Cheese

Red pepper and green pepper add an extra splash of color. (Pictured on page 84.)

1 8-ounce package block
   mozzarella cheese *or*
   Monterey Jack cheese
1 cup salad oil
½ of a medium sweet red
   pepper *and* ½ of a
   medium green pepper,
   seeded and cut into strips
2 tablespoons white wine
   vinegar
1½ teaspoons crushed red
   pepper
1½ teaspoons dried oregano,
   crushed
1½ teaspoons whole green
   peppercorns, crushed
½ teaspoon dried thyme,
   crushed
1 clove garlic, halved

● Using the tines of a fork, prick the block of cheese so the marinade will penetrate. Cut the block of cheese into ½-inch cubes. Place the cheese cubes in a 1-quart container with a tight-fitting lid. Set container aside.

● For marinade, in a small saucepan stir together salad oil, sweet red pepper, green pepper, wine vinegar, crushed red pepper, oregano, peppercorns, thyme, and garlic. Cook and stir mixture just till heated through. Remove from heat, then cool. Pour the oil mixture over the cheese in the container. Cover and shake gently. Marinate cheese and peppers in the refrigerator for 1 week before using, shaking container occasionally.

● To serve, let the mixture stand at room temperature for 30 minutes. Using a slotted spoon, transfer cheese and peppers to a small serving bowl. Pass as a salad accompaniment. To store cheese and peppers in the marinade, refrigerate, tightly covered, for up to 1 month. Makes 2 cups.

Parmesan Croutons

Be sure to make a double batch. You'll find it hard to keep from snitching these flavor-packed bread cubes. (Pictured on page 84.)

¼ cup butter *or* margarine
1 large clove garlic, minced
¼ cup grated Parmesan
   cheese
5 slices white, whole wheat,
   or pumpernickel bread,
   crusts removed and cut
   into ½-inch cubes (about
   3¾ cups)

● In a skillet melt butter or margarine. Add garlic and cook for 1 minute. Remove from heat. Stir in Parmesan cheese. Add bread cubes, stirring until cubes are coated with butter mixture.

● Spread bread cubes in a large shallow baking pan. Bake in a 300° oven for 10 minutes. Stir, then continue baking for 10 to 15 minutes more or till bread cubes are dry and crisp. Cool completely before using.

● To store, refrigerate, tightly covered, for up to 1 month. Bring to room temperature before serving. Transfer to a serving bowl and pass as a salad accompaniment. Makes 2 cups.

Italian Croutons: Prepare the Parmesan Croutons as directed above, *except* stir ½ teaspoon *Italian seasoning* into the butter or margarine mixture.

Dill Croutons: Prepare Parmesan Croutons as directed above, *except* omit the garlic and the Parmesan cheese. Stir 1 teaspoon dried *dillweed* into the melted butter or margarine.

Salad Buffet Party

It's time for a party! For a change in entertaining, delight your guests with a choice of main-dish salads. One of the recipes in this chapter, the Salad Bar Platter, even lets your friends create their own salads. (See recipes, pages 90–93.)

Putting the party together
This menu will serve 16. Your guests will choose from three salads and two soups. For smaller gatherings, trim the number of menu selections; perhaps choose only two of the salads, and one of the soups and breads.

Whether you're entertaining on your own or joining forces with others, you'll spend less time in the kitchen and more time with your guests if you follow a timetable.

Keep last-minute preparation to a minimum. Try to prepare as many of the recipes as possible in advance. For example, make the breads ahead and freeze them until the day of the party. Prepare the salads and soups several hours beforehand.

Tortellini and Spinach Salad
(see recipe, page 91)

Quick Tarragon Rolls
(see recipe, page 92)

Anadama Breadsticks
(see recipe, page 93)

Fruited Chicken Salad
(see recipe, page 90)

Make dessert time easy by serving ice cream and your favorite bakery cookies. Scoop the ice cream into paper bake cups earlier in the day and freeze them until serving time. Or, after everyone is done eating, take the tub of ice cream out of the freezer and let your guests serve themselves.

On the day of the party
Set the buffet table in logical order. Start with the plates, silverware, salads, and breads, then follow with the soups and iced tea. Use large plates for the salads and cups for the soups. That way, guests can place the cups on their plates for easy carrying.

Keep table decorations simple. A tablecloth and fresh flowers add a garden-fresh ambience.

MENU

Salad Bar Platter
Fruited Chicken Salad
Tortellini and Spinach
  Salad
Easy Vegetable Soup
Creamy Cheese Soup
Quick Tarragon Rolls
Anadama Breadsticks
Iced tea with lemon
Strawberry ice cream
Your favorite cookies

Easy Vegetable Soup
(see recipe, page 91)

Creamy Cheese Soup
(see recipe, page 92)

Salad Bar Platter
(see recipe, page 90)

Salad Bar Platter

It's like having a salad bar at home.

6 cups torn mixed greens
10 ounces sliced cooked beef, cut into 2½-inch-long strips (2 cups)
1 cup cherry tomatoes, halved
⅔ cup sliced fresh mushrooms
⅔ cup sliced cucumber
½ cup bias-sliced carrot
½ of a small red onion, sliced and separated into rings
Alfalfa sprouts
Sunflower nuts
Canned garbanzo beans, drained
Croutons
Assorted salad dressings

● In a very large mixing bowl combine greens, beef, tomatoes, mushrooms, cucumber, carrot, and onion. Toss lightly to mix. Cover and chill till serving time.

● To serve, transfer salad mixture to a large platter or 2 smaller platters. Let guests make their own salads by topping individual servings of salad mixture with sprouts, sunflower nuts, garbanzo beans, and croutons, and by choosing their favorite salad dressings. Makes 6 servings.

Fruited Chicken Salad

If you're entertaining outdoors, keep your salad chilled by setting the salad bowl in a foil-lined basket filled with crushed ice.

⅔ cup mayonnaise *or* salad dressing
2 tablespoons brown mustard
1 tablespoon brown sugar
1 clove garlic, minced
1 11-ounce can mandarin orange sections, drained
1 15¼-ounce can pineapple slices (juice pack), drained
4 cups cubed cooked chicken
1 cup thinly sliced celery
½ cup chopped green pepper
Chinese cabbage leaves *or* romaine leaves
1 3-ounce can rice noodles *or* chow mein noodles, *or* 1 cup chopped peanuts

● For dressing, in a small mixing bowl combine mayonnaise or salad dressing, mustard, sugar, and garlic. Stir till well blended. Cover and chill.

● Meanwhile, reserve 6 orange sections for garnish. Quarter the pineapple slices. In a large mixing bowl combine remaining orange sections, pineapple, chicken, celery, and green pepper. If desired, cover and chill for up to 4 hours.

● For salad, pour the dressing over the chicken mixture. Toss mixture lightly to coat.

● To serve, line a large salad bowl with Chinese cabbage or romaine leaves. Transfer chicken mixture to the bowl. Garnish with the reserved orange sections and some of the noodles or peanuts. Set out the remaining noodles or peanuts as a salad accompaniment. Makes 4 to 6 servings.

Tortellini and Spinach Salad

Combine salmon, spinach, and tortellini for a delicious, colorful salad.

1 7-ounce package cheese-
  filled tortellini
⅓ cup salad oil
¼ cup lemon juice
1 tablespoon Dijon-style
  mustard
½ teaspoon salt
¼ teaspoon pepper
1 clove garlic, minced
6 cups torn spinach
15 ounces cooked salmon* *or*
  one 15½-ounce can red
  salmon, drained, skin and
  bones removed, broken
  into chunks, and chilled
1 cup pitted ripe olives,
  drained and cut in half
2 green onions, thinly sliced

● Cook tortellini according to package directions, then drain. Place tortellini in a large salad bowl.

● Meanwhile, for dressing, in a screw-top jar combine salad oil, lemon juice, mustard, salt, pepper, and garlic. Cover and shake well. Pour dressing over warm tortellini. Toss lightly to coat. Cover and chill about 2 hours, tossing the mixture occasionally.

● For salad, add spinach, salmon, olives, and green onions to tortellini-dressing mixture. Toss lightly to coat. Serves 6.

*For 15 ounces of cooked salmon, start with 3 fresh *or* frozen *salmon steaks,* cut ¾ to 1 inch thick (about 1½ pounds total). Thaw salmon, if frozen. In a medium skillet combine 1 cup *water,* 1 tablespoon thinly sliced *green onion,* 1 *bay leaf,* ¼ teaspoon *salt,* and dash *pepper.* Bring to boiling; add salmon. Reduce heat. Cover and simmer for 5 to 10 minutes or till salmon flakes easily with a fork. Drain and cool salmon slightly. Then remove skin and bones. Break the salmon steaks into large chunks. Cover and chill before using in the salad.

Easy Vegetable Soup

Good homemade flavor without the fuss.

4 14½-ounce cans beef broth
1 16-ounce can tomatoes,
  cut up
2 large carrots, thinly
  bias sliced (about 1¾
  cups)
1 small zucchini, sliced
  ½ inch thick (about 1 cup)
1 stalk celery, sliced
  ½ inch thick
1 small onion, chopped
½ teaspoon dried rosemary,
  crushed
1 cup shredded process Swiss
  cheese *or* Gruyère cheese
  (optional)

● In a slow electric crockery cooker combine the beef broth, *undrained* tomatoes, carrots, zucchini, celery, onion, and rosemary. Cover and cook on low-heat setting for 8 to 10 hours (or on high-heat setting about 4 hours) or till vegetables are tender.

● To serve, ladle soup into cups or bowls. If desired, sprinkle with cheese. Makes 10 (1-cup) servings.

Creamy Cheese Soup

We used sharp American cheese during taste testing to get a cheesier flavor.

¾ cup finely chopped onion
¼ cup finely chopped celery
3 tablespoons butter *or* margarine
⅓ cup all-purpose flour
1 14½-ounce can chicken broth
2 cups shredded American cheese
3 cups light cream *or* milk
Popped popcorn (optional)
Snipped parsley (optional)

● In a large saucepan cook onion and celery in butter or margarine over medium-low heat till vegetables are tender but not brown. Stir in flour, then add broth. Cook and stir till thickened and bubbly. Cook and stir for 1 minute more. Then add cheese. Stir till cheese is melted. Remove from heat. Stir in cream or milk. Cover and chill overnight. (Or to serve immediately, heat soup just till warm.)

● To serve the next day, reheat soup over medium-low heat about 20 minutes or just till warm. *Do not boil.* If desired, top with popcorn and parsley. Makes 6 (1-cup) servings.

Quick Tarragon Rolls

No need to knead these rolls. The mixer does the work.

2½ cups all-purpose flour
1 package active dry yeast
1 tablespoon snipped parsley
1 teaspoon dried tarragon, crushed
1 teaspoon celery seed
1 cup warm water (115° to 120°)
2 tablespoons sugar
2 tablespoons cooking oil
½ teaspoon salt
1 egg

● In a large mixer bowl combine *1½ cups* of the flour, yeast, parsley, tarragon, and celery seed. In a small mixing bowl combine water, sugar, oil, and salt. Add water mixture to flour mixture, then add egg. Beat with an electric mixer on low speed for ½ minute, scraping sides of bowl constantly. Beat 3 minutes on high speed. Using a spoon, stir in as much of the remaining flour as you can to make a soft dough. Cover and let rise in a warm place till double (about 30 minutes).

● Spoon batter into 12 greased muffin cups, filling each slightly more than half full. Cover and let rise till nearly double (about 25 minutes). Bake in a 375° oven for 15 to 18 minutes or till lightly browned. Transfer rolls from muffin cups to a wire rack to cool. Makes 12.

Anadama Breadsticks

An inspiration from New England, molasses adds a slightly sweet accent to these breadsticks.

1¾ to 2¼ cups all-purpose flour
¼ cup yellow cornmeal
1 package active dry yeast
⅔ cup milk
3 tablespoons molasses
2 tablespoons shortening
½ teaspoon salt
1 egg white
1 tablespoon water
  Sesame seed *or* poppy
    seed

● In a large mixer bowl combine ¾ *cup* of the flour, cornmeal, and yeast. In a saucepan heat milk, molasses, shortening, and salt just till warm (115° to 120°) and shortening melts, stirring constantly. Add milk mixture to flour mixture. Beat with an electric mixer on low speed for ½ minute, scraping sides of the bowl constantly. Beat for 3 minutes on high speed. Using a spoon, stir in as much of the remaining flour as you can.

● Turn dough out onto a lightly floured surface. Knead in enough of the remaining flour to make a stiff dough that is smooth and elastic (8 to 10 minutes total). Shape dough into a ball. Place in a lightly greased bowl, then turn once to grease surface. Cover and let rise in a warm place till nearly double (about 50 minutes).

● Punch dough down. Turn out onto a lightly floured surface. Divide dough in half. Cover and let rest 10 minutes. Roll out each portion to form a 10x7-inch rectangle. Cut each portion into 24 strips (each 7 inches long and about ⅜ inch wide). Using 2 strips of dough for each breadstick, twist strips together and pinch ends together to secure. Place onto a greased baking sheet. Cover and let rise in a warm place till nearly double (about 30 minutes).

● In a small bowl combine egg white and water. Brush mixture onto unbaked breadsticks. Sprinkle with sesame seed or poppy seed. Bake in a 375° oven for 10 to 15 minutes or till golden. Transfer breadsticks to a wire rack to cool. Makes 24.

Freezing Rolls And Breadsticks

Your freezer can be a helping hand when you're preparing for this salad buffet party. The Quick Tarragon Rolls and the Anadama Breadsticks can be made up to 4 months in advance.

After the breads have cooled, wrap them in *heavy* foil or put them into freezer bags. Then seal, date, and label the packages. To thaw, open one end of each package, leaving the rolls or breadsticks inside. Thaw at room temperature about 30 minutes. Or reheat in foil in a 300° oven about 10 minutes.

Index

For the page numbers of our delicious low-calorie recipes, see the special category at the end of this index. Calorie counts also are given.

A-B

Aioli Platter, 54
Anadama Breadsticks, 93
Asparagus-Brats Toss, 22
Avocado and Seafood Salad, 35
Basic Vinaigrette, 80
Beef
    Beef and Vegetable Plates, 45
    Beef with Basil Dressing, 45
    Corned Beef 'n' Cabbage
      Salads, 69
    Layered Fiesta Salad, 46
    Mediterranean Salad, 15
    Orange 'n' Kiwi Salad, 17
    Salad Bar Platter, 90
    Steak Salads, 59
    Stir-Fried Beef Salad, 15
    Taco Salads, 67
Breadsticks, Anadama, 93
Brown Bagger's Salad, 23
Bulgur Salad in a Pocket, 40
Buttermilk Dressing, 85
By-the-Seashore Salmon
    Shells, 75

C-D

Cabbage
    Brown Bagger's Salad, 23
    Chicken, Noodle, and
      Cabbage Slaw, 59
    Chicken Pocket
      Sandwiches, 24
    Corned Beef 'n' Cabbage
      Salads, 69
    Slim Chicken Slaw, 29
Cheese Macaroni Salad, 18
Cheese, Marinated, 87
Cheesy Apple Salad, 42
Chicken
    Chicken and Fruit Toss, 73
    Chicken, Noodle, and
      Cabbage Slaw, 59
    Chicken 'n' Walnut Puff, 71
    Chicken-Orange Salads, 48
    Chicken Pocket
      Sandwiches, 24
    Chicken Salad on Melon, 49

Chicken *(continued)*
    Chicken Salad Tacos, 24
    Chicken-Spinach Salad, 26
Cod-Spinach Salad with
    Lemon-Mustard Dressing, 37
Cold Cuts
    Brown Bagger's Salad, 23
    Create-a-Chef's Salad, 20
    Deli-Style Pasta Salad, 20
    Easy-Serve Salad Rolls, 67
    Marinated Antipasto
      Salads, 60
    Prosciutto and Fruit
      Salads, 48
Coral Dressing, 82
Corned Beef 'n' Cabbage
    Salads, 69
Crab and Kiwi-Fruit Salads, 34
Creamy Cheese Soup, 92
Creamy Cucumber
    Dressing, 86
Create-a-Chef's Salad, 20
Croutons
    Dill Croutons, 87
    Italian Croutons, 87
    Parmesan Croutons, 87
Curried Salad-Stuffed
    Artichokes, 74
Curried Seafood Salad, 32
Curry Dressing, 82
Deep-Dish Salad Pizza, 70
Deli-Style Pasta Salad, 20
Dill Croutons, 87
Dill 'n' Chive Dressing, 86
Dressings
    Basic Vinaigrette, 80
    Buttermilk Dressing, 85
    Coral Dressing, 82
    Creamy Cucumber
      Dressing, 86
    Curry Dressing, 82
    Dill 'n' Chive Dressing, 86
    Herb Vinegar, 79
    Homemade Mayonnaise, 82
    Horseradish-Mustard
      Dressing, 82
    Low-Cal Blue Cheese
      Dressing, 85
    Low-Cal Italian Dressing, 80
    Nut-Flavored Oil, 79
    Orange Vinegar, 79
    Raspberry-Mint Vinegar, 80
    Thousand Island
      Dressing, 85
    Tomato Vinaigrette, 80

E-F

Easy-Serve Salad Rolls, 67
Easy Vegetable Soup, 91
Egg-Chard Toss, 40
Egg Salad in Tomato Tulips, 76
Fennel-Chicken Salad, 28
Fish and Seafood
    Aioli Platter, 54
    Avocado and Seafood
      Salad, 35
    By-the-Seashore Salmon
      Shells, 75
    Cod-Spinach Salad
      with Lemon-Mustard
      Dressing, 37
    Crab and Kiwi-Fruit
      Salads, 34
    Curried Salad-Stuffed
      Artichokes, 74
    Curried Seafood Salad, 32
    Gazpacho Salad with
      Shrimp, 32
    Gingered Shrimp Salads, 53
    Lasagna-Wrapped Salmon
      Salad, 62
    Minted Pea-and-Fish
      Salad, 38
    Paella Salad, 31
    Rice Stick and Shrimp
      Salads, 51
    Salmon and Melon Salad, 38
    Scandinavian Greens, 31
    Seafood-Pear Salads, 52
    Seviche Salad, 60
    Shrimp-Rice Ring, 64
    Spring Greens Salads, 52
    Super Salad Bowls, 54
    Sweet-and-Sour Pasta
      Salad, 34
    Tortellini and Spinach
      Salad, 91
    Tossed Salade Niçoise, 36
    Tuna and Pasta Salad, 36
    Tuna-Orange Toss, 37
    Tuna-Stuffed Tomatoes, 75
Fruits
    Chicken and Fruit Toss, 73
    Chicken Salad on Melon, 49
    Crab and Kiwi-Fruit
      Salads, 34
    Fruited Chicken Salad, 90
    Gourmet's Delight, 49
    Papaya Boats with
      Chicken, 71

Fruits (continued)
Poultry-Filled Summertime Melons, 73
Prosciutto and Fruit Salads, 48
Salmon and Melon Salad, 38
Seafood-Pear Salads, 52

G-H

Garden Potato Salad with Ham, 17
Gazpacho Salad with Shrimp, 32
Gingered Shrimp Salads, 53
Gourmet's Delight, 49
Grape and Pork Salad, 19
Greens
Avocado and Seafood Salad, 35
Cheesy Apple Salad, 42
Chicken 'n' Walnut Puff, 71
Chicken-Spinach Salad, 26
Cod-Spinach Salad with Lemon-Mustard Dressing, 37
Create-a-Chef's Salad, 20
Curried Seafood Salad, 32
Deep-Dish Salad Pizza, 70
Egg-Chard Toss, 40
Fennel-Chicken Salad, 28
Grape and Pork Salad, 19
Layered Fiesta Salad, 46
Lots-of-Layers Picnic Salad, 51
Mediterranean Salad, 15
Orange 'n' Kiwi Salad, 17
Oriental-Style Chicken Salad, 28
Rice Stick and Shrimp Salads, 51
Salad Bar Platter, 90
Scandinavian Greens, 31
Seviche Salad, 60
Sizzling Cheese Salad, 56
Sparkling Strawberry-and-Poultry Salad, 26
Spring Greens Salads, 52
Steak Salads, 59
Stir-Fried Beef Salad, 15
Taco Salads, 67
Tortellini and Spinach Salad, 91
Tossed Salade Niçoise, 36

Greens (continued)
Tuna-Orange Toss, 37
Wilted Lettuce with Chicken, 30
Herb Vinegar, 79
Homemade Mayonnaise, 82
Horseradish-Mustard Dressing, 82
Hot Potato and Bratwurst Salad, 22

I-N

Italian Croutons, 87
Lamb
Mediterranean Salad, 15
Tabbouleh with Lamb, 19
Lasagna-Wrapped Salmon Salad, 62
Layered Fiesta Salad, 46
Lemon-Marinated Olives, 86
Lemony Chicken-and-Broccoli Salad, 29
Lots-of-Layers Picnic Salad, 51
Low-Cal Blue Cheese Dressing, 85
Low-Cal Italian Dressing, 80
Marinated Antipasto Salads, 60
Marinated Cheese, 87
Meatless
Bulgur Salad in a Pocket, 40
Cheesy Apple Salad, 42
Egg-Chard Toss, 40
Egg Salad in Tomato Tulips, 76
Sizzling Cheese Salad, 56
Teriyaki Tofu Salad, 62
Three-Bean and Cheese Salad, 42
Tortellini and Parsley-Pesto Salad, 41
Mediterranean Salad, 15
Menu, Salad Buffet, 89
Minted Pea-and-Fish Salad, 38
Nut-Flavored Oil, 79

O-P

Olives, Lemon-Marinated, 86
Orange 'n' Kiwi Salad, 17
Orange Vinegar, 79
Oriental-Style Chicken Salad, 28

Paella Salad, 31
Papaya Boats with Chicken, 71
Parmesan Croutons, 87
Pasta
Asparagus-Brats Toss, 22
By-the-Seashore Salmon Shells, 75
Cheese Macaroni Salad, 18
Deli-Style Pasta Salad, 20
Lasagna-Wrapped Salmon Salad, 62
Sweet-and-Sour Pasta Salad, 34
Tortellini and Parsley-Pesto Salad, 41
Tortellini and Spinach Salad, 91
Tuna and Pasta Salad, 36
Pork
Cheese Macaroni Salad, 18
Easy-Serve Salad Rolls, 67
Garden Potato Salad with Ham, 17
Gourmet's Delight, 49
Grape and Pork Salad, 19
Pork and Papaya Salads, 46
Prosciutto and Fruit Salads, 48
Vegetable Ham Medley Salad, 18
Poultry
Brown Bagger's Salad, 23
Chicken and Fruit Toss, 73
Chicken, Noodle, and Cabbage Slaw, 59
Chicken 'n' Walnut Puff, 71
Chicken-Orange Salads, 48
Chicken Pocket Sandwiches, 24
Chicken Salad on Melon, 49
Chicken Salad Tacos, 24
Chicken-Spinach Salad, 26
Deep-Dish Salad Pizza, 70
Easy-Serve Salad Rolls, 67
Fennel-Chicken Salad, 28
Fruited Chicken Salad, 90
Gourmet's Delight, 49
Lemony Chicken-and-Broccoli Salad, 29
Lots-of-Layers Picnic Salad, 51
Marinated Antipasto Salads, 60

Index

Poultry *(continued)*
  Oriental-Style Chicken
    Salad, 28
  Paella Salad, 31
  Papaya Boats with
    Chicken, 71
  Poultry-Filled Summertime
    Melons, 73
  Salad Bundles, 25
  Slim Chicken Slaw, 29
  Sparkling Strawberry-and-
    Poultry Salad, 26
  Tabbouleh with Lamb, 19
  Wild Rice with Duck
    Salad, 23
  Wilted Lettuce with
    Chicken, 30
Prosciutto and Fruit Salads, 48

Q-Z

Quick Tarragon Rolls, 92
Raspberry-Mint Vinegar, 80
Rice
  Curried Salad-Stuffed
    Artichokes, 74
  Paella Salad, 31
  Rice Stick and Shrimp
    Salads, 51
  Shrimp-Rice Ring, 64
  Vegetable-Ham Medley
    Salad, 18
  Wild Rice with Duck
    Salad, 23
Rice Stick and Shrimp
  Salads, 51
Rolls, Quick Tarragon, 92
Salad Bar Platter, 90
Salad Buffet Menu, 89
Salad Bundles, 25
Salmon and Melon Salad, 38
Scandinavian Greens, 31
Seafood-Pear Salads, 52
Seviche Salad, 60
Shrimp-Rice Ring, 64
Sizzling Cheese Salad, 56
Slim Chicken Slaw, 29
Soup, Creamy Cheese, 92
Soup, Easy Vegetable, 91
Sparkling Strawberry-and-
  Poultry Salad, 26
Spring Greens Salads, 52
Steak Salads, 59
Stir-Fried Beef Salad, 15

Super Salad Bowls, 54
Sweet-and-Sour Pasta Salad, 34
Tabbouleh with Lamb, 19
Taco Salads, 67
Teriyaki Tofu Salad, 62
Thousand Island Dressing, 85
Three-Bean and Cheese
  Salad, 42
Tomato Vinaigrette, 80
Tortellini and Parsley-Pesto
  Salad, 41
Tortellini and Spinach
  Salad, 91
Tortilla Bowls, 67
Tossed Salade Niçoise, 36
Tuna and Pasta Salad, 36
Tuna-Orange Toss, 37
Tuna-Stuffed Tomatoes, 75
Vegetables
  Aioli Platter, 54
  Beef and Vegetable Plates, 45
  Garden Potato Salad with
    Ham, 17
  Gazpacho Salad with
    Shrimp, 32
  Gingered Shrimp Salads, 53
  Hot Potato and Bratwurst
    Salad, 22
  Lemony Chicken-and-
    Broccoli Salad, 29
  Marinated Antipasto
    Salads, 60
  Minted Pea-and-Fish
    Salad, 38
  Steak Salads, 59
  Super Salad Bowls, 54
  Teriyaki Tofu Salad, 62
  Three-Bean and Cheese
    Salad, 42
  Vegetable-Ham Medley
    Salad, 18
Wild Rice with Duck Salad, 23
Wilted Lettuce with Chicken, 30

Low Calorie
(Calories per serving)

Chicken and Fruit Toss
  (271), 73
Chicken-Orange Salads
  (368), 48
Egg-Chard Toss (271), 40
Egg Salad in Tomato Tulips
  (182), 76

Fennel-Chicken Salad
  (338), 28
Gazpacho Salad with Shrimp
  (249), 32
Low-Cal Blue Cheese
  Dressing (25 calories/2
  tablespoons), 85
Low-Cal Italian Dressing
  (3 calories/2
  tablespoons), 80
Poultry-Filled Summertime
  Melons (298), 73
Scandinavian Greens
  (253), 31
Seviche Salad (185), 60
Slim Chicken Slaw (301), 29
Tuna-Orange Toss (183), 37

Tips

A Vinegar for Every Taste, 78
Easy-to-Make Garnishes, 44
Freezing Rolls and
  Breadsticks, 93
Identifying Salad Greens, 8
Kitchen Cut-Ups, 58
Oil Options, 78
Selecting and Handling Salad
  Greens, 6
Serving Containers, 44
Sprout Gardening in a Jar, 66
Super-Easy Marinating, 58
Two Ways to Cook Chicken
  for Salads, 66
What's a Cup?, 14

When you're looking for a light and refreshing taste in food, turn to BETTER HOMES AND GARDENS. *All-Time Favorite Salad Recipes* and *Eating Light* cookbooks. You'll find both books are packed full of recipes using the freshest of ingredients.